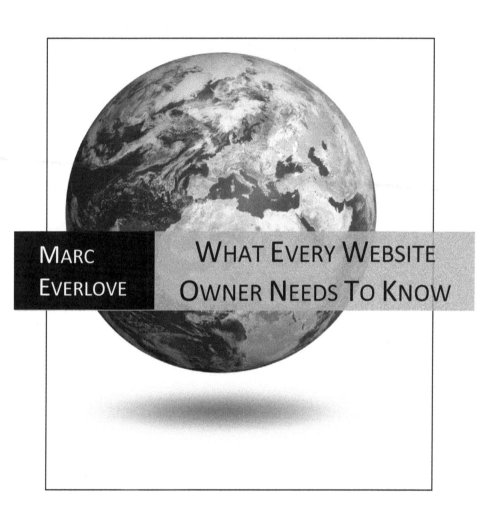

MARC
EVERLOVE

WHAT EVERY WEBSITE
OWNER NEEDS TO KNOW

COPYRIGHT

ISBN-13: 978-0-557-33527-5

This book is dedicated to:

Lauri, Adam & Rachael, Courtney and Drake

for believing the impossible can happen,

& more importantly, believing in me.

DISCLAIMER

The information contained in this book has been obtained by the author from sources believed to be reliable. However, because of the possibility of human or mechanical error by the author, his sources, or others, the publisher, nor author does not guarantee the accuracy, adequacy, or completeness of any information and is not responsible for any errors or omissions or the results obtained from use of such information. Readers should be particularly aware of the fact that the Internet is an ever-changing entity. Some facts may have changed over the course of time since this book went to press.

ACKNOWLEDGEMENTS

I owe a great deal of thanks to everybody that has been so helpful during the creation of this book.

Thank you, Lauri, my beautiful and wonderful wife, for giving me the support and time to make this book a reality. Without you I am sure it would still be a box of notes somewhere.

Thank you, to my kids Rachael & Adam, Courtney and Drake for understanding and always being supportive. You guys are the best kids a guy could hope for and that is saying a lot!

A special thanks to Edward McGrath for the inspiration and the knowledge that helped bring this from simple musings to the book that you now hold in your hands.

Thanks also to Pards Productions and M.MAC Clothing for all they have done.

Also to all of my clients and the great people with whom I have done so much business with over the years.

Thank you all and God Bless!

–Marc Everlove

ABOUT MARC EVERLOVE

Marc Everlove is a Microsoft Certified Systems Engineer and a Microsoft Certified Database Administrator. Previously the Director of Information Technology at the South Bay Association of REALTORS®, He is currently an independent consultant with Evermore Technology. He currently resides in Southern California with his wife Lauri and two of his three children Courtney and Drake. His eldest daughter recently married and lives in Minnesota with her husband Adam.

FOREWORD

I have chosen to self publish this book. It is my first book with many (hopefully) to follow. I tried to write it as if I were speaking directly to you. Please excuse and report any errata you may encounter. Unfortunately, my skills in the language arts are such as they are...

Of course, this book is born out of my observation that there are a lot of people who need websites, but do not have enough information to get started, or are unaware of what they need to do to find success online.

With that in mind, I set out to write this book in hopes that I can clarify some of the mystery that surrounds the process of publishing a website. My goal here is not to provide the technical aspects of web development, but rather, to give the layperson a general understanding of the process so that they may be start out with a bit of knowledge.

With that said, I hope that I have done my job in relaying this information to you well. There is a lot to know and much of it is difficult to put into words. Therefore, if you have any questions or comments I encourage you to register on my website www.EverMoreTech.com and leave your thoughts on the community forum. I will get back to you as soon as I am able.

WHO SHOULD BUY THIS BOOK?

*T*his book has been designed and written for ordinary, non-technical people who are either planning to have a Website created or already own one. Even though, I will explain the basics and the fundamentals of how websites work and how to build them, I am assuming that a professional Webmaster will be used to actually create the Website.

This book is intended to give non-technical people a clear, concise understanding of what they need to have a successful online presence. After many years of creating Websites for ordinary, non-technical people, the need for this book has become very clear. It can help equip the average business person with the knowledge and tools necessary to be a successful Website owner.

If you are like most people; you probably don't want to become a computer engineer, you would rather spend the time running your business and a Website is simply a part of that. Whether the most technical thing that you ever want to deal with is a doorknob, or perhaps, you are ahead of the curve, this book can help you get the most out of your site. In any case, running a successful website is full of nuances, pitfalls, and secrets. This book can help unravel these mysteries and lead you to successful Website ownership.

Developing Websites, I have worked with a great many people from all walks of life. Some didn't know the first thing about technology, while others were extremely adept and practically all skill levels in between. Through this experience I have compiled a list of topics that every website owner should know about. You will find them here.

This book will cover a wealth of secrets, tips and information about Website ownership, from step one, the very early stages of Website ownership, all the way through search engine optimization and marketing. Finally, I will give you a few tips on keeping your Website up-to-date and filled with current content to keep your visitors coming back for more!

WHAT EVERY WEBSITE OWNER SHOULD KNOW

1. KNOW WHERE & HOW TO GET INFORMATION
2. DON'T OVER-THINK IT
3. KNOW THE BASICS
4. HOW BROWSERS WORK
5. DOMAIN REGISTRARS
6. WEB HOSTING
7. ALL HOSTS ARE NOT CREATED EQUAL
8. WHAT THE HECK IS HTML ANYWAY???
9. FILE TRANSFER PROTOCOL: FTP
10. USER NAMES & PASSWORDS
11. WEB DESIGN PROGRAMS
12. WHAT IS WYSIWYG
13. CROSS BROWSER/PLATFORM COMPATIBILITY
14. WEB DESIGNER OR WEB DEVELOPER
15. CHOOSING THE RIGHT WEBMASTER
16. COMMUNICATING WITH YOUR WEB DEVELOPER
17. LAYOUT AND DESIGN
18. GRAPHICS AND LOGOS
19. ANOTHER HELPING OF HTML
20. SCREEN RESOLUTION
21. ADA COMPLIANCE
22. DIFFERENT TYPES OF WEBSITES
23. W3C COMPLIANCE
24. FORMS, SCRIPTS & LANGUAGES

25. FRAMEWORK & PLATFORM WEBSITES

26. PROFESSIONAL GRAPHICS & PHOTOS

27. MAINTENANCE

28. TRADITIONAL MARKETING

29. GUERRILLA MARKETING

30. SEARCH ENGINE OPTIMIZATION

31. GOOGLE ADWORDS

32. BLOGGING

33. ONLINE COMMUNITIES

34. FREEBIES, TOOLS AND OTHER ONLINE GOODIES

35. BLACK & WHITE; HACKERS AND THEIR HATS

36. SPAM, SCAMS & HOW TO PROTECT YOURSELF

37. GENERATION X & Y; THE WEB SAVVY CUSTOMER

38. PDAS, NOTEBOOKS, CELLS & MOBILITY

39. WEBMASTER TOOLS & OTHER USEFUL THINGS

40. REDESIGN, UPDATES, UPGRADES & KEEPING FRESH

MARC
EVERLOVE

WHAT EVERY WEBSITE OWNER
SHOULD KNOW

CHAPTER ONE

KNOW WHERE & HOW TO GET INFORMATION

So, you have decided; for whatever reason, you need to have a presence on the Internet. Obviously, this means getting a website. If you are like the majority of people on this planet, you probably have little or no idea where to start. Considering the cost of building a professional, successful website, you may be facing a significant investment. To make matters worse; unless you are fortunate enough to have an I.T. department, you are probably at square one with nowhere to go for reliable advice...

> *"Know Where and how to get information..."*

Well there is no need to worry, you have already started. Between the information contained in this book and the information which you can find on my website www.EverMoreTech.com you are well on your way to having all the tools and information you will need right at your fingertips. *Just being prepared will help your odds of success significantly.*

Whether you intend to build your website yourself, or if you are planning to have a professional build it for you; having a good foundation of knowledge is extremely important when you start out. With the basics that are covered in this book you will have a good fundamental understanding of how Websites work, the tools needed to create them and how to launch, maintain and market them. This can mean the difference between success and failure.

Congratulations, you have taken the first step toward owning a successful Website! Even though it may be as simple as picking up this book, you have started down the path to having your own online presence. Additionally, you now know that you are not alone. You know the first thing that every website owner should know: Where to start, where to get information, and soon you will know how to use it. Even better, the rest of the book is pretty easy too. So sit down, make yourself comfortable and let's get to the meat and potatoes. You might want to grab a pen, or pencil because I've included several blank pages and many places that you can take notes directly in this book that will help you organize your thoughts and store information that you will need to keep handy throughout the entire process.

CHAPTER TWO:

DON'T OVER-THINK IT

*K*eep it simple. You've probably heard it said a thousand times before, regarding a thousand different topics, but it really applies here. A common misconception many people make is to assume that publishing and running a Website is some kind of mystical process, in which only ultra-geeks, with super human intellect can do. While I would love to consider myself to have any superhuman attributes whatsoever, sadly, I don't. Nope, not even close.

I do not want to give you the wrong impression. There is a lot to learn and it can get confusing. However, if you take your time and you are patient, you can do it. It is a simply a matter of taking it one step at a time and making sure you understand what you are learning as you go.

Don't worry about knowing everything; just play heads up ball. By having a good grasp on the fundamentals, a firm understanding of the basics, you can make good decisions. Making good decisions is a key factor in running a successful website. Leave the technical details to the experts. If you know what you want, let the techies worry about how to make it work. If you can do this, then you will make everybody's job easier.

Technology changes, but the concepts don't. Fortunately, your job is not to be an expert at technology; you just need to manage it to get the results that you want. Easy as pie... In fact; your job is a manager, or overseer. You are in charge and your Webmaster is trying to make you happy. Do both of you a favor and make it easier for him.

Therefore, if you stick to your vision and work to communicate that vision, then you can maintain your focus on the big picture. Leave the nuts and bolts to your Webmaster. If you have picked a good one, he will work to make your vision a reality.

One of the most important things you need is an overall basic understanding and a clear vision of what you want to accomplish with the website and a general idea of how you think it should look. If you don't know exactly what you want, then spend a couple of hours surfing the Web. Take notes regarding what you like and what you dislike.

> "Your likelihood of success largely depends on your follow through... When the website is finished, your work is just starting."

If you do not have a clear idea of what you want, how can you expect your webmaster to know? By spending some time planning, communicating and organizing you will help minimize the amount of changes the website will need later on and generally speed up the process. This will also help the website to appear professional and well thought out.

The amount of technical expertise needed to be a successful Website owner is actually quite minimal.

However, this largely depends on the resources available. As with any aspect of business; it is a trade-off; money vs. knowledge & time. The more you know and the more time you are willing to spend on it, the less it will ultimately cost. Inversely, the larger the budget that you can allocate toward the site will allow your webmaster to include more resources, such as: a development team, graphic artists and images, animators, web applications and other useful tools. In either case, you can launch a terrific website, if you are willing to do what it takes.

Regardless of the budget you can dedicate toward your website, if you want to be truly successful, there are a number of things that are absolutely essential to know. This is where many Website owners fail. Do not be alarmed; most of it is more common sense in nature, rather than technical.

For instance: many website owners assume that once their website is launched the teaming masses will clamor to visit and the money will just start rolling in. Many owners will completely neglect marketing altogether. Sometimes lightning strikes and every now and then a Website is an overnight success right off the bat. Don't depend on it though.

> ### THE TOOL BOX
>
> *Evermoretech.com contains a companion section to this book. You will find the code and other items that I discuss in this book there.*
>
> *Additionally, there are many other tools and tips that are updated and maintained regularly. By bookmarking it and visiting it regularly, you will remain informed. .*

Most likely, it will take time, money or sweat equity, a bit of "know how" and a little effort.

Now, for the good news: just by the simple act of reading this book you are ahead of the game. Many aspiring Website owners are completely in the dark regarding the whole process. The lack of knowledge necessary to launch and maintain a successful website leaves a website owner completely dependent on their Webmaster. While there are some good Webmasters out there, it is perhaps not the strongest position to be in. By educating yourself you have placed yourself at the front of the class and improved your chances of success substantially...

> "Even though all of this may seem overwhelming, if you take it one step at a time, you will get there."

Many less technically inclined people have made the mistake of believing that the whole process of launching a Website is more difficult than it really is. Often people will believe that they have to be a computer guru, or that it is harder than it is. Often, this apprehension gets the better of them and they never start or they abandon a Website that they paid good money to get online because they do not know what to do next. I have seen some very nice (and expensive) Websites suffer this fate; in fact, often the website never even gets completed. This can be extremely frustrating for everyone involved.

In some cases, the prospective website owner will freeze like a deer in the headlights when all that is required of the prospective owner is a few simple paragraphs about their business, or perhaps a photo or two. The frustrated Webmaster contacts them several times requesting the information, but never receives it. Eventually he stops trying, and finishes the site to the best of his ability without the desired information. Of course, the site ends up being less than it could be. In other cases, simply a bit of marketing after the website is completed would suffice.

If the owner of the failed site simply had kept an open mind, a good webmaster would have been happy to work through the rough spots step by step. Ultimately the owner would have spent a few short hours scribbling a handful of paragraphs. In many cases, the owner simply needs to take twenty minutes to look over a site and give some suggestions. It makes a lot of difference.

Cases like these are prime examples of why you should spend the time to plan and organize your thoughts. By being prepared, you will be ready and make the entire process run smoothly.

These people were no less intelligent than others I have worked with and I have taught people with all sorts of different skill sets. You don't need to be a tech-wizard to do this. Regardless, they convinced themselves that it was harder than it really is and paid the price.

The bottom line is this, if you are not willing to invest even the barest minimum of time and effort, your site will suffer for it. Therefore, I recommend that you approach technology with an open mind and don't assume anything.

Consider this, regarding technology; kids generally "catch on" the quickest. While there are many reasons for this, I believe this is largely due to the fact that they simply approach computing with an open mind. Furthermore, it is apparent to me, that one secret to children's success with technology is due to the fact that they accept it for what it is, rather then what they expect it to be. They are able to simply learn by trial and error, as opposed to dealing with preconceived notions.

If you want to improve your general computer skills quickly, then I recommend finding a game, or application that you enjoy and have fun with it. Once you can do that, the rest will come intuitively.

CHAPTER THREE

KNOW THE BASICS!

It is a good idea to have a basic knowledge of how the Internet works. I don't mean the in depth nuts and bolts, but rather a basic overview. This will help you understand the different processes that are at work and how you can use them to your benefit. If you look at it from the correct perspective, it is surprisingly easy.

Nerd Note

There are many different types of network traffic. Some is one-way (such as UDP) and some is two way (like TCP).

Two-way traffic is similar to certified mail. Upon receipt of the packet a response is sent back indicating that the packet was received. One-way traffic such as IP or UDP is simply sent without verification.

The Internet is simply a large network of computers. Anyone can connect to it with the right equipment and it is available virtually anywhere on the planet. It is just a system of millions of computers communicating with each other.

Each computer or device on the Internet (or almost any network for that matter) has its own unique address (Just like your house). This is known as an IP (Internet Protocol) address. IP addresses are what are used to route data. When you type www.something.com into your browser the domain name is translated into an IP address.

23

The US Postal Service is a great analogy to use to describe how the Internet works:

Let's say you wanted to get in touch with my dear old Aunt Mildred. You can send a letter to Aunt Mildred who lives in Wisconsin from practically anywhere on the planet. At least anywhere that you can find a mailbox (Oh and don't send cash of course ...).

Mildred's address is unique. She lives at 123 Main St. Anytown, WI 98127. The postal system decodes her address and then routes the letter to the post office nearest Mildred. From there it is sorted further and is placed on a mail truck and eventually it is delivered to her door. Since there is only one address, the mail ends up where it is supposed to be, you can see where there would be a huge problem if there were identical addresses.

All of the information flowing across the Internet has been broken down into little packets and each packet has the destination address and return address in the header. A simple email message can be broken down into millions of packets and each packet finds its way to the destination computer where it is rebuilt into its original format. This all happens at the speed of light. Think of it as sending each piece of a jigsaw puzzle through the mail separately.

In simplest terms TCP/IP is the addressing system every computer on the Internet uses. The Internet "postal system" is known as DNS (Domain Name Service). The DNS system is made up of millions of servers all over the world. There only job is to resolve domain names to IP addresses. While it doesn't sound like a big job, Billions and Billions of requests are made every hour. TCP/IP and DNS are the backbone of the Internet.

The genius of the system is that it is distributed across the globe. In fact, if you so desired, you could run a DNS server yourself. Fortunately, you don't have to; in most cases it makes sense to let an outside company handle hosting your website.

I know this is a lot to throw at you early on in the book and that it is relatively complicated. You don't need to commit this to memory however. It is a concept that will need to be familiar with. Later on, we will look into this a bit further. It will all make more sense when we start looking into purchasing your domain name (i.e. whatever.com). For now, just let it percolate in your mind.

CHAPTER FOUR:

HOW BROWSERS WORK

So, what exactly is a **browser** anyway? While that may seem like a stupid question, obviously it is what you use to get on the Internet, but, have you ever really thought about it? Of course, you know what it is basically, but what about a little more in-depth? How do they work and why?

These are just a few of the major questions people have, but don't want to ask.

So, let's break this down:

When you open your browser (Internet Explorer, Firefox, Safari etc ...) and visit a Website, this is what happens:

1. When a user, we'll call him Joe, opens a browser, he is launching a very powerful program. Even though you might not think of your browser as a program, it is exactly that.

2. Joe types www.EverMoreTech.com into the address bar and presses Enter.

3. The request for that Web page travels out over the DNS system.

4. Eventually (actually, at light speed) it reaches the **Web hosting server** that actually hosts the web page.

5. The hosting server processes the request and then breaks the file into millions of small data packets and sends them back over the Internet to the Joe's computer. These packets are then rebuilt and placed in all of the correct order on Joe's machine and sent to his browser.

Now, here's where the fun begins; the web page that you see is not what was sent over the Internet. Actually, a simple text file containing HTML source code was sent. This source code is the equivalent of an architect's blueprint.

Your browser acts similarly to a house-builder and interprets these "blueprints" and assembles the Web page accordingly. Any images, graphics or other files that may be needed are then downloaded.

However, just as builders are not created equally, browsers have differences as well (see the Nerd Note).

Nerd Note

If two builders are given the same set of blueprints, the structures that they build could be quite a bit different, this is due to differing interpretations of the blueprints..

*Likewise, different browsers will assemble Web pages differently. Some browsers conform to web standards and some do not. **Standards Based Browsers** all produce the same overall results, while **Non-Compliant Browsers** do not necessarily conform to the "rules" of Web design.*

*This is known as **cross browser compatibility.***

You should make certain your site looks presentable in any of the major browsers.

Currently, the most popular browser is Microsoft's Internet Explorer (there are several versions in parentheses). Several rival browsers, Firefox, Chrome and Safari are gaining market share quickly. This is significant because it is the browser that "assembles" the Website based on the "blueprints" (the HTML code) provided by the web server and because each browser may interpret these "blueprints" differently, there may be significant differences in the results.

When you are deciding on a Webmaster, be sure to consider this and make sure that ***cross browser compliance*** will be tested!

CHAPTER FIVE

DOMAIN REGISTRARS

*D*omain Names are the first step to launching a Website. Once you have made the decision to launch a Website, the obvious first step is to pick out and secure a good domain name. This is done by visiting a ***Domain Registrar.*** Most registrars have a tool on their Website that lets you check to see if a domain name is available or not. If you find one that you like, then it is a relatively easy process to purchase it.

A Registrar will provide ***Name Servers*** that will enable your Website to be available online. I am not referring to being "found" by a person using a search engine, which is a subject we will get into later. I am referring to having your domain physically available online.

> # Nerd Note
>
> A ***Name Server*** is a computer that resolves your domain name into an ***IP Address.*** Essentially, this is what allows you to simply type *EverMoreTech.com* instead of *68.183.185.191.*

Name Servers and what they do, seem to cause a lot of confusion amongst many website owners, particularly when changing web hosts, registrars or webmasters. Frequently, the owner does not know the password/user combination, or even worse, the name of the actual registrar. This can cause quite a bit of extra work and slightly delay your project. Therefore, make certain to keep this information safe. In most cases your Web host will send you an email containing all the information that you will need. Be sure to print out a copy and keep in your records.

If your Webmaster sets up your hosting account, be sure to have him forward you a copy of the login information I mentioned above.

*A decent Webmaster should be able to find the name of the registrar easily, but if you have changed email addresses then it can be more difficult. Even though in most cases you will be able to access it once you prove that you are the actual owner, it is a hassle that is easily avoided if you make sure to record your domain registrar account information.

Congratulations! Once you have set up a domain name, you are officially a Website Owner (see, that wasn't so hard, was it?). However, at this point, that may not mean much; due to the fact that your Website probably just points to a *"parking page"*. This page is automatically put in place by your domain registrar. It may have a few ads on it, or perhaps nothing at all. *Regardless, it is your Website and nobody else can use that domain name while you own it.*

Each domain name is completely unique. There can only be one. However, keep in mind the fact that there are several different **Top Level Domains** or **TLDs** (.com, .org, .biz, etc ...). Each TLD is independent of the other TLDs. Any domain name may be registered by separate companies or individuals, regardless of the desires of the other Website owner's wishes. This means that if you own widgets.com, someone else can come along and register widgets.org and still another person or company can be the owner of widgets.net and so on.

There have been many unfortunate cases where a Website owner has registered a domain name and subsequent registration of the same domain name with a different TLD has been purchased by a competitor or worse. If an "opposing domain name is either fraudulent, or a competitors domain, your marketing efforts may be sending your clients to their Website. How would it reflect on you or your business if the .net, .biz, .org, or other version of your domain name belonged to a competitor that did poor work, or just had a poorly built Website up... What if it was a rip-off scheme, or porn?

For this reason, it may be important for you to register all of the major TLDs for your domain name. This depends on whether you believe that there may be competition for your domain name. If your competition buys the .org and the .net version of your domain name and publishes a competing Website there, it could be problematic for you.

$ $ $ $ $ SCAM ALERT! $ $ $ $ $

Beware of Domain Name Renewal Scams:

Many unscrupulous domain registrars exist. It is a common practice of these registrars to send official looking letters in the mail, or email messages informing you that your domain is about to expire. This may or may not be true.

Though it may not say outright in the letter, they will typically have the appearance of being either your current registrar (they assume you don't know who that actually is), or even from the Government or some other official office. The tone of the message is usually urgent and in some cases may allude to a fine, or some vague penalty if left unpaid.

In reality, these registrars have nothing to do with either the government, or your current registrar. They are simply looking for people that don't know how this all works.

They will include a form to send along with a checkbox to "renew" your domain name. If the form and a check are sent in, then the unscrupulous registrar will transfer your domain name from your current, legitimate *registrar to their company.*

The bogus registrar is now the official registrar for your domain name.

Sometimes this will have little or no impact on your services, while other occasions, the "new" registrar may have inferior equipment, services, or be located in part of the world that has poor infrastructure. If this is the case, then your website may load slowly, erratically, or not at all.

Even worse, it may be difficult to contact them due to international hours or poor customer service. Depending upon the company, it may be difficult to transfer control away from them and back to a more reputable registrar.

Additionally, some of these registrars charge big bucks for registrations and will also charge for transfers. They (even some of the more reputable companies) are not in a hurry to lose your revenue.

Fortunately, there are better measures in place to ensure the safety of your domain name. Many registrars lock your domain name and require you to unlock it before it can be transferred to another registrar.

DOTCOM FAUX PAUX

Think it can't happen? Www.WhiteHouse.gov is the official site of the Office of the President of United States of America. Www.WhiteHouse.com was/is a pornography site. You can imagine the embarrassment this created in Washington. Despite the federal government's best attempts to stop it, a judge ruled that it was completely legal.

Still not convinced? Some years ago a young Web designer (a high school student) named Mike Rowe registered (yes, you guessed it); www.MikeRoweSoft.com. He gained some notoriety and quickly received an offer of $500.00 from Microsoft. He replied in a letter with a counter offer to sell the name for $10,000.00. Microsoft then sent a strongly worded cease and desist letter threatening legal action. The Microsoft Lawyers in Redmond were apparently not amused. By this time, the media and bloggers got wind of the story and MikeRoweSoft.com got so much traffic (and support) that it crashed his hosting companies Web server and they told him he they couldn't handle the demand. Another Webhosting company stepped up and offered him hosting at no charge. The bad publicity of Microsoft strong arm tactics vs. a high school kid caused the Microsoft company to back off. I believe they came to some kind of settlement.

If you are ready to take the plunge, it is time to visit a Domain Registrar and pick out a domain name. There is no time like the present and your domain isn't going to register itself. The sooner you get started the better. The competition for domain names is a lot like the land rush in the early days of this country. There are still many good domain names to choose from, but every day that goes by, hundreds of thousands of new domain names are registered.

The sooner you start the better chance you will have of getting a domain name you are happy with. Not to mention; the longer a Website has been in existence (and the length of time it is registered for) is a factor that determines how high search engines will rank your pages.

Just visit www.EverMoreTech.com/DomainName for a list of registrars, user's experiences & ratings of their services, prices and links. Of course, I encourage you to leave your own opinions.

You will also find a tool on my site that will allow you to see if your desired domain name is available or not (most registrars will have similar tools).

One last thing before you go rushing off to buy your first domain name; take a few moments to think about it. Chances are, if you are in a popular field, there may not be much to choose from, but if you are clever, you should be able to come up with something that you are happy with.

When you are choosing a domain name here are a few things to keep in mind;

- Keep it short. The longer the domain name is, the greater the chance that your potential visitors will make typos, misspellings, or simply be too lazy to type ThisIsMyReallyCoolDomainName.com.

- Avoid tricky spellings, homonyms, puns, or other gimmicky names. Unless this is really a prominent part of your business branding, I caution against using alternative spellings and or substituting characters (i.e. using the number 3 as a substitute for the letter E, this is known as "Leet") unless your target audience is a young cyber-literate group such as gamers. Using alternative spellings can cause confusion and be difficult to tell someone over the phone.

- While it may be unavoidable, try to keep letters such as S & F, B & V, or D & T etc ... to a minimum. When you are trying to give your Website address (particularly over the phone), or someone needs to jot down your e-mail address, it can be a challenge to make sure they get it.

- Use a .com TLD if you can. I try to use .com where ever possible. The .com top level domain is the most recognizable and will generally be the default when someone types in your domain name without it into a search engine.

- Keep it simple

- Allow for growth —if you choose BooksBooksBooks.com you are limited to books, whereas if you go with something more general such as; BooksAndMore.com you have room for growth if your site takes on a new direction previously unforeseen. If your site is specific to an industry and will not change, you may want to disregard this, but that is up to you.

- When possible, get something that is easy to remember. This is important. How many times have you sat down to the computer and could not think or a particular website's name?

- Write down 30 good names. Then, cross out ten. Number the remaining 20 and visit a registrar to see if any of your favorites. If at first you don't find one that you are thrilled about, or none of your favorites are available, then relax, and try again.

- If you can't decide between a few different domain names, you can get them all and simply point, or forward all of them to your Website. Most registrars will allow you to forward a domain name for free.

Once you have the domain name that is right for you; GRAB IT! More than once I have waited to buy a domain name only to find it was taken by the time I made up my mind. With that said; be careful checking out. Some Registrars attempt to sell you everything from so-called traffic boosters to the kitchen sink on your way to the credit processing page. JUST GET THE DOMAIN NAME! I do not recommend purchasing the add-ons particularly the $1.99 hosting package ... I will talk more about Web hosting in the next chapter.

CHAPTER SIX

WEB HOSTING

*C*ongratulations, in just a few short pages you have covered lot of ground. You know what registrars do and you understand what name servers are, it's time to talk about ***Web hosting***. Web hosting is simply the term applied to the process of publishing your website to the Internet; therefore, it's no surprise that a Web host is a provider of Web hosting services.

To elaborate; a Web server is a computer connected to the Internet that runs a special application (the actual Web server application) that "listens" to the Internet for a request for a Web page, file or other resource contained on

> ### HEY LOOK, A CLUE!
>
> *The difference between a **server** and a **computer** ...*
>
> *A server is actually software. There are many different types of server software for many different tasks. Web servers, DNS servers, file servers etc ... In a nutshell, a server is an application that is meant to perform a task for a group of people or networks. Due to the nature of server software it is common to dedicate a computer to run it. It is also common to run many different server programs on the same computer. Considering this, the computers running server software had to be very powerful so computers began to be built for this specific purpose, hence becoming known as "servers". So essentially the only difference between a server and a computer is the software that is*

one of the Websites the Web server controls. It then sends the appropriate information back over the Internet to the computer the requested it.

That's all there is to it. It is not magic, the Internet doesn't just "run", it is made up of millions and millions of individual Web servers.

You should look for a hosting company that offers you services that will best suit your needs. Some hosts will offer and faster computers and/or faster connections (bandwidth), others will offer an array of different features and web space, while others will offer a rock bottom price. Depending upon the needs of your Website, how much content you plan to include; particularly; high quality graphics, audio (**Podcasts**), video (**Vodcast**) and other large, bandwidth intensive files and applications, will determine what kind of hosting package that you need.

Web Hosting Features Demystified

Just what is a redundant fiber backbone with multiple ISPs and why do I need it anyway?

When you are searching for a Web host and comparing the different features offered, there are some terms used to describe the different features. Understanding what these terms mean and what your needs will likely be, can save you a considerable sum of money later on. I realize that a lot of this stuff is about as exciting as watching grass grow, but you will be glad you did later.

Most average sites do not require more than one or two *Gigabytes* of Web space (This will undoubtedly change in time).

You do not necessarily need the most expensive plan. If you find that you need more, than it is usually a simple matter to request an upgrade to a better plan.

Some basic features to be concerned about:

- **Web space** *–This determines how much content you will be able to store on your site.*

- **Bandwidth** *–This is a measure of the data you can send over your site per day/week/month.*
- **Server performance** *–Faster machines mean better performance...*
- **Backups** *–Are the servers (and your Website) backed up daily?*
- **Access** *–Do you have the access you need? In most cases a simple control panel and* **FTP** *access should do the trick*
- **Support** *– Is there a toll free number? Is the support 24/7?*
- **Streaming videos, podcasts, webinars, or other media** *–Support for streaming media may be an additional add-on, or included in a premium package.*
- **SSL** *–Security Certificate necessary for ecommerce sites.*
- **Physical Security** *–does the facility have 24/7 security?*

Websites that offer high quality video, audio, photos, graphics, or have excessive traffic will use more resources than an average site. Sites that accept credit cards will need **SSL** to provide secure payment transactions. Corporate sites may need a ***dedicated server***. Business may want to use ***co-location*** etc...

In order to launch a successful Website you will need to keep your start up and operating costs manageable. Future considerations such as marketing, maintenance, and redesign can be costly. Assuming the hosting services you choose are adequate for your needs, the less money you spend on hosting the better. I mention this because there are many hosts that will charge top dollar for a level of service you do not need. Don't get cheap, unreliable service, mind you, just be aware that you don't need to overpay. The more money you can save on hosting, the more you will have for other aspects of your site.

BEYOND THE BASICS

There are many other more advanced options and features that you may need. Your Webmaster should know which features he will require. Chances are he will have a Web host that he uses routinely. By using a single Web host he will be familiar with the control panel and features of that particular provider. This will save time and prevent issues regarding compatibility.

On the other hand, he may be a reseller (which is common) and have a vested interest in selling you the most expensive package you can afford. As long as you know what you are getting into you are in good shape. A little knowledge can go a long way to save you money in this business.

In any case, a few questions up front can go a long way to making your Website a success. If you simply ask him

WHAT EVERY WEBSITE OWNER NEEDS TO KNOW

if he has any special needs or preferences, if he has a Webhost that he has good experiences with and if he is affiliated with that Webhost.

Some advanced features to consider:

Platform Type – This indicates the type of server your site will be hosted on. There are 3 commonly used platforms. Microsoft®, UNIX and Linux.

Programming Language Support –There are many different languages that your Website may be written in. Before selecting a Web host I recommend discussing this with your Webmaster. He may have some requirements regarding the language he prefers to program in. Asp.net, Ruby and PHP some of the more commonly used languages on the Web today. *Light* scripting languages are also used, such as JavaScript and VBScript.

Databases –There are various types offered, the most popular are MySQL, MS SQL, Oracle & Access. If your Website is being written in PHP then you will most likely use a MySQL Database, while if your Webmaster writes in ASP.Net than MS SQL, or Access will most likely be the databases of choice.

Shopping Cart –If you are planning an E-Commerce site, or are planning to sell anything, you will probably want a shopping cart. Many web hosting companies offer free shopping carts, or shopping carts as an add-on feature.

Dedicated Server –If your website is large, gets a lot of traffic or has special needs, you may need your own server. Many web hosts offer dedicated or managed servers that exclusively run your website.

WHADDYA MEAN "WHAT 'S MY PASSWORD?"...

From time to time, it may be necessary to transfer a website from one company to another. Frequently, the owner does not have the registrar or the **FTP** login information. The Registrar login information is needed to administrate the domain name and the FTP login information is necessary to transfer the files to and from the Web host.

Usually, this is not a problem. However, if the original Webmaster can no longer be contacted, there can be trouble. There can be no transfer until account access has been restored. If the owner is not listed as the administrative contact, proving ownership of the domain name may be difficult. In most cases it can be squared away, but it is rarely fun and easily avoided. All you have to do is write down your information in the "Important Info" Appendix at the end of this book.

"Most webmasters spend hours researching web hosts and over the years will have evaluated many potential hosts and should be able to make some recommendations.

Bottom line —*Make sure that you are listed with the registrar as the administrative contact and you have all account information BEFORE you need it and keep the login information in a safe place.*

DO IT YOURSELF WEB HOSTING? YE BE WARNED...

Eventually, you will hear or read somewhere that you can enable the **Personal Web Server (PWS)** and run your own Web server. You might be thinking "Gee, can save a few bucks and host my site for free". While this is true, and may even seem easy, this is a huge endeavor if you want to do it properly.

TURN BACK NOW, WHILE YOU STILL CAN!

If you are still determined to run your own Web server here are a few things to consider:

- **Security:** With millions of hackers, viruses, worms, spyware packages, exploits and other Internet threats, security is a paramount. While this applies to all computers; it is even more vital for a Web server. Web servers are extremely vulnerable simply due to their accessibility. A web server must have certain **ports** open to communicate with other computers. This adds a whole new level to complex security issues.

  To deal with the added security requirements and vulnerabilities, you will need a good hardware firewall, properly configured. Furthermore, the server must be set up properly and "patched" regularly so no exploits that could allow a hacker, worm, or other malware access are left open. You will also need to monitor the security logs for any suspicious activity on a daily basis.

- **DNS**: if you're going to run your own web server then you will need to run a public DNS server, or find a third party service to run your DNS zone for you. This is beyond the scope of this book

- **Static IP address**: you will also need a static IP address so that your domain name will resolve to your Website. As we discussed before an IP address is what networks use to locate and identify other networks, computers and other Internet enabled devices. A static IP is usually more expensive than a dynamic IP. The difference between a static and a dynamic IP is simply this; a static IP never changes it is always a particular address such as 68.183. 185.191 versus a dynamic IP that will change either periodically, or every time you turn on your computer. With this being said it is possible to run a Website with a dynamic IP address by using a third party company, however I do not recommend this approach.

- *Mail server:* assuming you want to receive e-mail through your domain (i.e. you@yourdomain.com) you will need to install and configure a mail server on your computer and all the goes with it. By doing this you are enabling the service on your computer called *SMTP* (simple mail transport protocol). By turning on SMTP you have just open yourself to becoming an unsolicited e-mail relay server, better known as a *spam zombie*. And in properly secured and configured SMTP server will allow anybody on the Internet to use your computer to send e-mail. Even worse than that, with a few easy to get programs available widely on the Internet, they can even make these emails appear to be coming directly from you.

If this isn't enough to scare you off, and you are determined to run your own Website, then I hope you'll visit my website www. EverMoreTech.com. I have some tips and tricks as well as more detailed and in-depth instructions and advice to do this properly. However, I reiterate, it is cheaper be easier, more secure, and less of a headache to simply by hosting services. I personally run my own web hosting business and we'll be happy to host a Website for you at a reasonable price.

CHAPTER SEVEN

ALL HOSTS ARE NOT CREATED EQUAL

ow that you know a little bit more about web hosting, it is time to think about actually choosing a web host.

Services offered range from simple web hosting with no features, to comprehensive packages including templates, a marketing plan, search engine submission, and more.

Sometimes this can be confusing for a prospective website owner. Too many choices can lead to what may not be the best decision. Therefore, one of the most important things to consider is reliability. Regardless of what else is offered, or how great the deal is, if your website is down half the time, it's not worth it.

> "Remember, your Website is an online representation of you and your business.
>
> Therefore, it is important to choose wisely."

After reliability, email is probably the next critical feature you should consider. Before you sign up with a hosting company, you can check to see if their mail servers appear on any **black lists** (Just visit my website to find out how to do this.). Additionally, most web hosts offer protection against spam. It will also allow you to add email addresses that you want to make certain you receive email from to a **white list**.

Spam filtering is a balancing act. The higher the security, the less spam will get through, but the greater the probability that legitimate email is filtered along with the junk mail. Depending upon how important you consider your email, will determine your "comfort level" regarding spam filtering.

MAKING THE CHOICE

Choosing a Web host is an important step and should be done carefully. If you choose a substandard service your Website may be unacceptably slow and/or unreliable.

The quality of Web hosting services varies a great deal depending on the provider. A Web host provider can range from a small startup hosting business consisting of a single web server, all the way up to state-of-the-art data centers and everything in between. Smaller companies may be not be able to offer the same service and reliability, while large companies might be

HEY LOOK, IT'S A CLUE!

Beware of Inferior Webhosts...

- *If the provider does not have enough bandwidth your site will load slowly.*

- *If the provider does not have redundant connection your site will not load if there is a problem with the Internet connection.*

- *If the provider's security is too restrictive your Web applications may not work properly.*

- *If the provider does not have adequate backup; you could lose the site altogether, so make sure you have your own.*

These are just a few of the possible calamities that can happen. After the blood, sweat, tears and money that you have gone through to get your site up, a good Web host is essential. You will know you have a good Web hosting company if you never have to think about them once the site is up.

too restrictive making it difficult to work with their security.

If you visit my website, www.EverMoreTech.com I have included a list of reliable web hosting providers, what they offer, and a tool in which you can compare them. You'll also find updated lists of the type of hardware that should be expected from any decent web host.

CHAPTER EIGHT

OK, SO WHAT THE HECK IS HTML ANYWAY?

The basic language of the web is something known as HTML. It is the format in which instructions are sent over the Internet. HTML provides us with a light, flexible language that allows us to transmit large amounts of information effectively and efficiently.

It is due to HTML that different types of computers and operating systems can all read the same Web pages and communicate with each other effectively. Actually, there is a lot more to it all then just plain HTML, but for the average Web site owner, you will not be expected to know about the nuts and bolts of Web development. For your purposes suffice to say; HTML allows any computer with an appropriate browser to surf the net.

It is not imperative that you know HTML, but it can help you communicate with your Webmaster. For this purpose, you should probably read this chapter. However, if techno speak makes your hands sweat, or you already know HTML, then it is safe to skip this chapter...

HTML stands for Hypertext Markup Language. Although similar, HTML is not actually a programming language. It is much, much simpler. Comparing HTML to a programming language is like comparing a soap box racer to a Porsche... A fully fledged programming language is capable of doing much, much more than basic HTML.

HTML is a set of tags that modifies text. In simpler terms, HTML is basically a set of instructions that tells browsers how to assemble the Web page.

An HTML file is simply a plain text file that is saved with an .htm or .html file extension. In addition to the plain text, the .htm file contains the HTML tags I mentioned earlier. When your browser receives the .htm page it interprets the tags and formats the text accordingly.

This is accomplished by enclosing HTML tags in angle brackets. This way the browser "knows" that anything enclosed in angle brackets is an HTML tag. For example <b> is the HTML tag that instructs the browser to bold the text that follows it. An angle bracket followed by a slash would signify the end of a tag. Therefore the text that is in between becomes a modified by that particular tag. Clear as mud?

It is really quite simple. HTML simply instructs the browser how to display text and images. That is all there is to it. No need to over think it... If you need some text to display in bold then you just use the <b> tag. When you no longer want the text bolded you add the </b> tag to close the original bold tag. Any text that is between those tags is bolded in the browser.

OK here's an example.

You see this in your browser:

The **quick** brown fox **jumped** over the lazy dog.

The underlying HTML would look like this:

```
The<b>quick<b> brown fox <b> jumped</b>
over the lazy dog.
```

Some tags format text, others that allow you to display images, tables, lists and other structural elements. There are even more that will allow you to add more powerful scripting languages and other elements to your website. We will look more in depth at this later on. Even with all of the different things you can do, it all boils down to using tags to modify simple text.

Look at it this way... Every word in the English language is comprised of twenty-six simple letters right? Once you master those letters, look what you can do. Similarly, with a handful of HTML tags you can work wonders and once you understand the basics you can read just about any HTML code.

Cool, huh?

So you see it's really quite easy. Fortunately, you are a website owner and not a website developer. So you don't have to know everything there is to know about the HTML, just the basics. In other words; you don't have to *know* HTML, you just have to *know about* HTML. If you take the time to learn a little bit more than you need to know, then you are really ahead of the game.

This chapter will explore basic HTML and I will provide an appendix at the end of this book of basic HTML tags. Most of them are relatively self explanatory and you will know what they mean right when see them, but a good "Short List" of common HTML tags can really come in handy.

So let's take a more detailed look shall we? Now that you see just how simple HTML really is let's take a look at a basic HTML page.

As you've just learned an HTML page is nothing more than simple text modified by various tags set in angle brackets. Although it is not always necessary, it is good form to begin any HTML page with the HTML tag and end the page with the closing HTML tag.

So it should look like this:

```
<html>

This would be the content of your page.

</html>
```

Obviously, a little bit more than the above code makes up your average web page. The HTML tag at the beginning of the page is important because it helps the browser to understand what language the page is written in (HTML pages can have several other languages included as well). Usually, in a simple HTML page the head tag would follow the HTML tag. Inside of that head tag you will in most cases find a title tag. The title tag is the tag that controls the text that is at the very top of the browser when you open it. There may be some other code nested in the head tag, but we won't be concerned with that now.

Here is an example of the code:

```
<html>

<head>

<title> my very first web page</title>

</head>

</HTML>
```

See now, it's easier than it looks, isn't it? The above code will produce a blank web page titled my very first web page. I am guessing however, you already figured this out.

Before I continue, I would like to reiterate; you do not have to remember all of this. This information is just to give you an understanding of what HTML is and how web pages work. Besides I have included the handy list of common HTML tags at the end of the book...

Of course, now that you know how simple it is, you may want to experiment with it. You do not even have to buy

Nerd Note

*A **Text Editor** is similar to a word processor but much simpler. A word processor, such as **Microsoft's Word** saves invisible formatting information along with the text that modifies it (sound familiar?). To write HTML you will need to use a program that does not add anything to your code. Text Editors do not use any formatting and save in **ASCII**.*

*Notepad is included with all versions of **Microsoft Windows**, while **SimpleText** or **TextEdit** are included with the **Apple OS** depending on the version.*

anything. HTML can be written in any text editor. It simply has to be saved as either an .htm or an .html file.

Let's take a further look at this. The following code will render a very simple web page. As we continue to add different elements I will explain exactly what's happening. First we will start with the code that we used above and add to it. To actually add content, we will need to add a body tag. The body tag will contain your content (no surprises here...). It tells the browser that the following content is to be displayed.

If you would like to follow along, I encourage you to do so. The source code for this project is available online, so you can simply copy and paste it into Notepad. You will find it on my Website at *www.EverMoreTech.com* under the *"books"* section.

Now, in your text editor (for which we will use Notepad as an example) click *"File"* and then *"save as."*

Open Notepad (or your any text editor *See note) type the following:

```
<html>

    <head>

    <title> my very first web page</title>

    </head>

    <body>

    This is my first web page.

    <p>

    <b>This text is bold.</b>

    </body>

    </html>
```

Next, Name your file: "first.HTM". Make sure to include the quotation marks.

Before you click *"Save"*, click the arrow next to the *"Save as Type"* field and select *"All Files"*.

This is an important step, if you do not select *"All Files"* as the file type, your file will be named first.htm.txt. This is a problem because the computer uses the letters after the dot (known as the file extension) to determine which program to use to open the file. So if

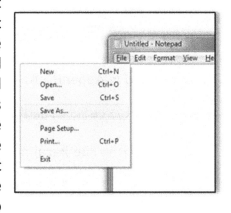

the computer sees a `.txt` at the end it knows your file is a text file and will use your default text editor to open it. However, if the file has `.htm` or `.html` as the file extension, the computer will use a browser to open it. In fact, the reason you should put the file name in quotations when you save is; just in case you forget to set the file type to "all". If the filename is in quotes, then it will save it exactly as typed regardless.

Congratulations, you have made a working web page.

Conclusion:

HTML is much simpler than you may have thought. It is something that you can probably learn to do quite well if you put your mind to it. Even though there are many expensive programs designed for professionals, all you need is a simple free text editor to get started. There are many tools on the web as well. You can find links to many at www.EverMoreTech.com. We will take a deeper look into HTML later on in the book and you can always stop my Website if you would like a more in depth hands on tutorial.

A FEW TAGS TO REMEMBER

Here is a short list of HTML tags that are commonly used. Another list is included later on and a comprehensive list is included in Appendix A.

`<html>` `</html>` —The HTML Tag

`<p>` `</p>` —The Paragraph Tag

▶ `<br />` —The Line Break Tag

▶ `<font>` `</font>` —The Font Tag

- o Attributes (attributes define different aspects of a tag)
    - Face —Determines the font face
    - Color —Determines the color of the text
    - Size —Determines the size of the text
- ▶ `<img src="YourFile.jpg">` —The Image Tag
    - o Attributes (Optional)
        - Height —Specifies Height
        - Width — Specifies Width
        - Border —Determines the size of the text
        - Align — Specifies Image Position

These basic tags are a few of the tags that make up the foundation of HTML. There are many others, but it is only essential that you have a basic understanding of HTML. The more you know and understand, the better you will be able to administrate your Website later on. In any case, if you choose, you can simply let your Webmaster worry about the code; it will be enough that you understand what is going on. However, a little time invested now, will almost certainly pay big dividends later.

I have included an appendix at the end of this book containing a more comprehensive list of HTML tags. Once you have mastered the basics, then you can move on to understanding and using more complicated techniques.

CHAPTER NINE

FILE TRANSFER PROTOCOL: FTP

ile transfer protocol is how you copy your Website files from your local computer to a Web server. Virtually all Web design applications have some form of FTP client that will allow you to transfer your files to the Web server. This is known as publishing your website.

Additionally there are standalone FTP programs that have no web developing capabilities whatsoever, but simply transfer files between your local computer and a Web server. In most cases the FTP client will require a username and password. However sometimes you can login as an anonymous user, although if you do you may not see all the files that would be available if you were actually an authenticated user.

Most likely, you will not have to worry too much about FTP at all. However, you should know about it in case you ever have to download your Website. Hopefully, this won't happen to you. In a perfect world, when you change Webmasters everything should go totally smooth without incident, problems, or other issues. However, this is reality and I have seen some "messy breakups" between clients and Webmasters.

Often, when a Website owner comes to me, they have had a bad experience with their prior Web designer. In some cases it was the kid next door, a daughter's boyfriend, or their friend's uncle's brother's cousin that was "really good with computers ". Inevitably, there was some sort of falling out; both parties are angry, frustrated and hostile. At this point the website owner and the previous Webmaster are no longer on speaking terms, but the Website owner does not have a copy of his website, nor does he have any of the password user names and is not in a terribly good position.

Nerd Note

There are programs available that will help you download your site even if you don't have the passwords. Generally, they do a pretty good job. However, it is better to have a copy of the original source code...

In these cases it is usually up to the new Webmaster to somehow get a copy the existing Website. Of course the hostile environment between my new client and his previous web developer is likely to spill over and create problems transferring the domain and the Website.

This is why I say it is of paramount importance that you know what FTP is and what is going on. Because if something like this should happen to you and you need a change Web hosts, developers, Webmasters, or whoever you have working on your site and things have "gone to the dogs" you should know what's going on.

From the start, make sure that you have the following information:

- Domain registrar, username and password
- Web host name, username and password

- If possible, a copy of the source code and database (of course this will not be available until the site is completed)

It is best to do this early before you have any problems. Hopefully, everything will go smoothly and there will be no issues, but consider it cheap insurance. It will only take your webmaster a couple of moments to burn a CD of all the source code for your website, but it will take you all whole lot of time, energy and trouble if you don't have it and your Webmaster gets hit by a bus.

As I said before, this probably won't happen to you. However, it happens enough that it warrants this chapter (Ok, maybe not the getting hit by a bus part, otherwise I would be in a different line of work.). Having said that, I have observed many problems that have occurred between Webmasters and clients have been caused by communication difficulties. The Webmaster/developer begins to speak non-technical terms, while the client goes along without completely understanding. At some point things turn sour.

In light of this, if you do not completely understand something, ask. Do not go forward until you understand what's going on. You'll be much happier if you spend a moment now to save the hours of aggravation later on.

A good Webmaster will understand that this is a difficult and foreign process to many non-technically inclined people and take the time to explain things until they are understood.

CHAPTER TEN

USERNAMES, PASSWORDS & ACCOUNTS

*E*ven though this seems like a simple topic, it isn't. Most people have misplaced or forgotten important login and account information at some point. Of course, this usually discovered at the worst possible time.

STRONG PASSWORDS

The first thing you should start thinking about is what exactly your username and password should be. Frankly, if you're at all concerned about security you should know that most passwords that are less than six characters long will only take moments to break. There are programs out there (which will remain nameless) that help hackers crack passwords.

HEY LOOK, A CLUE!

Guidelines for Strong Passwords

1. Use eight characters or more
2. Do not use passwords that can be found in the dictionary
3. Use uppercase and lowercase letters
4. Use numbers and symbols
5. Do not use birthdays, names or other things of a personal nature that can be guessed by somebody with a little information about you. You may be surprised how much information about you is floating around the public domain...

So the first thing that you need to keep in mind is whatever password that you choose needs to be very secure.

Even though it may be a pain in the neck to type a strong password, you will get used to it quickly and if you use it enough, you will be able to enter it relatively quickly.

Oddly enough; video games, bad grammar and poor translation have contributed to the creation of an ingenious method of creating strong, easy to remember passwords. 1337, also known as, Leet is the language of gamers and instant messaging. It is a simple substitution cipher in which numbers, symbols and improper spelling is substituted for letters. In other words Leet (short for elite, as in you have to be one of the Internet Elite to understand it) is spelled 1337. The one is a substitute for the letter "L", the three is a substitute for the letter "E", and the seven is a substitute for the letter "T".

There is no right or wrong way to spell or use grammar in Leet. For instance my name Marc could be spelled a number of ways such as:

- /\/\@2c
- ^^4|-<
- M42c

You see, there are not really any rules; you just have to be able to understand it. It gets quite in depth, but if you substitute even just a couple symbols for letters then you will have a password that is very easy to remember and very difficult to crack.

If you visit my website I have a table containing many of the different substitution characters for 1337 and links to quite a bit more information regarding this topic.

USERNAMES

Many user names are common. Usernames such as: admin, administrator, super user, host, developer, guest, owner, backup and other default names are extremely common. Hackers know this and often go to a Website and start with common username/password combinations. By simply using an uncommon username, you reduce the chances of getting compromised.

KEEPING TRACK

Creating, maintaining and remembering user account information can be simplified if you take a few moments to learn some good practices. After all, your login information is the frontline of security, isn't it worth the time to develop good habits? Odds are; you will be glad you did later.

There are a few ways to approach this issue; the last one is the only one I recommend...

1. **Use the same username and password for everything that you do online** –Even though makes it easy to remember your login information, if hacked or otherwise compromised, all of your accounts are vulnerable. The hacker may attempt to use the login information to access different sites commonly used by the public. For example: Banks, eBay, PayPal, online stock trading websites, credit unions etc... Whatever additional information gleaned can then be used to open new accounts and make fraudulent purchases.

2. **Write down login information** —Many users write their login information in a notebook or on a piece of paper in a drawer next to the computer. What's even worse, usually in this case accompanying the user names and passwords is the website that the username or password is used for. I have even seen this information on post-it notes sticking to the frame of the monitor! I do not recommend this practice. However, if this is the best method for you, I strongly encourage you to keep them in a secure location. Furthermore, if you add a bogus character to the password (and remember that you did!), even if it ends up in the wrong hands you are still safe. Better yet, just write down a clue.

3. **Keep them all in a document** —Many people keep text file, spreadsheet or other such file containing all their user names and passwords. Often, they keep it in a folder called passwords.

   Wow, this is really dangerous. This is like hitting the jackpot for a hacker. Not only is all of the login information in one place, but if the machine has been compromised then it may be available to any hacker that downloads the proper software. Don't be a victim be smart.

4. **Keep email messages** —Some people keep a folder in Outlook or an online email account with all their account information. While this is extremely convenient, if your account is compromised then all of your login information is in one nice tidy

place for the hacker. Outlook and free e-mail accounts are prime targets for hackers looking for just that sort of information. So again, I do not recommend this method. *I don't recommend this...*

5. **Security Levels & Ciphers** –An effective way to remember user names and passwords is to use various security levels and ciphers. If you have four or five different username/password combinations for various levels of security, you can effectively keep track, of all of them.

   For example, if your username is FuzzyBear you can have a corresponding password based on the level of security that you're looking for. Here are some examples of what I'm talking about below:

   a. For your favorite community forum you could use the username FuzzyBear with the password fumanchu

   b. For your account to your local library you could use the same username with a password fumanchu123

   c. For your computer account you could use the same username with the password FuManchu86

   d. For your online banking account you could use the same FuzzyBear0 and password FuM4nchu. FuM4nchu is fumanchu in 1337 as discussed above.

   I do recommend this. This keeps all of you sensitive login information in your head & it is relatively easy to remember. If you must write it down for safe keeping, fine, just make darn sure that you keep the information in a safe location.

There are some programs that store passwords and user names in an encrypted form that offer pretty good security. If you are hacked and the hacker gains access to these files, because they're encrypted, they cannot see the data. For list of these programs (some of which are free) you can visit my Website www.EverMoreTech.com. One thing to keep in mind though, if these programs are poorly written or exploits are found, then they can hand your login information over to hackers on a silver platter, so use them at your own discretion.

CHAPTER ELEVEN

WEB DESIGN PROGRAMS

$\mathcal{M}$any websites that will require ongoing maintenance once they have been completed. If this is the case with you, you may want to do some things on your own. This makes a lot of sense assuming that you are sufficiently technically competent.

However, it is important to know your limits, backup before your try anything new and implement changes on a test site before adding them to your production site. Additionally I strongly recommend having really good communication with your Webmaster before you consider doing anything of this nature. If

> **HEY LOOK, IT'S A CLUE!**
>
> **Keeping Up To Date**
>
> Things change quickly; you may want to visit EverMoreTech.com for any updated tools, tips, or information.

If you do plan on working on your site, you will probably want a good web development program. Some leading applications are Microsoft FrontPage™, Microsoft Expression Web™, Adobe Dreamweaver™ and a few others. If you visit my website you can find links to trial versions of all these and more.

I do caution you though. Unless you are sure about what you are doing and you can live with the consequences of crashing your site, then think twice about tweaking your site. There may be an alternative. Read on...

If you are intending to update the content and regular basis I recommend using a content management system. There are a few different solutions that may work for you. "Framework" Websites, Adobe Contribute and Template based Websites are a few that you may want to consider. We will get into more detail regarding these options later on in the book.

CHAPTER TWELVE

WYSIWYG VERSUS CODE

What you see is what you get, better known as WYSIWYG is simply the design interface of any web development application that shows what the site will look like. Virtually all web design programs today offer a WYSIWYG interface. Typically they will allow you to switch between the design interface and the code interface allowing you to work in a graphical environment as well as to manipulate the code directly. Additionally, they will usually have a split screen view that allows the designer to use both the code and the WSIWYG interface

While professional design and development applications may not be right for you, there are other applications that will allow you to add edit and delete content. Known as Content Management Systems these programs allow you to create and modify content in predefined areas. Content management systems offer a great deal of power and flexibility and control over your website. They are typically easy to use once you get the hang of it.

There are some downsides to content management systems of course. Cost can be a factor. Additionally, you will need to find a Webmaster that works with the program. Once you have gotten past those obstacles you will need to learn the application yourself.

Even though most content management systems are meant for casual users, there is still much to learn. If however, you are willing to take the time to learn, having the ability to make changes and alterations to your Website will be more than worth the effort. Most content management systems have modules interfaces are similar to Microsoft Word™ or any other word processor.

Content management systems are a must have if you intend update your website regularly. If you take the time to learn and actually use it, your rewards can be extremely fruitful. Not the lease of which; you will not need to rely on your Webmaster for simple changes.

"A good content management system will allow you to be more self-reliant which in the end if that means a little time and

Often a Website owner wants a simple change and because their Webmaster is busy he cannot change it in a timely fashion. Often these little changes are urgent for the client. Ultimately both the client and the Webmaster become frustrated. A good content management system will allow you to be more self-reliant which in the end if that means a little time and money it is worth it.

One more thing to consider is time. Websites can be tremendously time consuming. It is very easy to completely lose track of time when you are working on your site. This is particularly true when you are working on something new and challenging. When you really get into working on a Website, time loses all meaning; a few minutes can easily turn into an afternoon before you know it.

CHAPTER THIRTEEN

CROSS BROWSER/PLATFORM COMPATIBILITY

Cross browser compatibility is an important feature that you should be aware of. The majority of people currently use Microsoft Internet Explorer to view the web. There are however several different browsers on the market that also are used to view the web. Now if you'll remember; a web page is basically a set of blueprints that is assembled on your machine by a browser.

Each browser will interpret the code sent by a Web server a little differently. The World Wide Web consortium publishes guidelines that browsers are supposed to adhere to. These guidelines are known as the W3C Standards.

> **HEY LOOK, A CLUE!**
>
> **Cross Browser Compatibility**
>
> *Due to the differences in the way that rival browsers interpret the HTML the output is slightly different. In some cases it can be quite pronounced. It may break the page completely.*

Even though it is the most popular browser by far, Microsoft Internet Explorer is not really a standards based browser. Microsoft has taken liberties in interpreting code as well as allowing code which other browsers cannot read. Considering that the time of this writing Microsoft Internet explorer has an 80% market share you can see where this creates problems.

Internet explorer's chief rival is Firefox. Firefox has been gaining popularity recently and has enjoyed tremendous growth. A few years ago Internet explorer had about a 95% market share. As more users begin to migrate to other browsers such as Firefox, Opera, Safari, and others, cross browser compliance becomes a more important issue.

Make sure you download several different browsers and look at your Website in each one separately so you can see what other people see that are using different browsers.

Even though the 800lb. gorilla here is Internet Explorer there are several different versions and older versions do not display all of the bells and whistles of modern sites. The math is pretty simple. If 20% of your visitors are using something other than Internet Explorer, then out of every 100 visitors roughly twenty are going to be using a different browser other than Internet Explorer. If you get 100,000 visitors a month that means 20,000 visitors will be using a browser other then Internet explorer. If your site looks bad in some of those other browsers then you can bet you will look unprofessional to those users. Can your business afford to look unprofessional to 20,000 people?

There are some links to utilities that will allow you to see what your website will look like in various different browsers and screen resolutions (more about screen

resolutions   and   platforms   later)   at
www.EverMoreTech.com.

Chapter Fourteen

Web Designer or Web Developer?

ost people don't understand the different roles that different people play in the concept, design, development, deployment, and maintenance of the average Website. Obviously, Websites can vary in size and complexity from very small and simplistic to very large and comprehensive. Most basic Websites only require a third party Webmaster to keep their site up and running. Larger companies or companies that have more comprehensive needs have entire departments dedicated to maintaining their online presence. Let's not forget that more and more companies are emerging in which the entire company revolves around its Website.

Webmasters, designers, graphic artists and developers, not to mention various other Information Technology personnel, they are all different and they all have specific responsibilities.

Let's take a look at who these people are and what they do.

First, there's the Webmaster; he is responsible for day to day operations: collating, updating content and coordinating different departments in the case of large Websites. The Webmaster is also typically responsible for monitoring the Website, ensuring there are no broken links or other errata. Basically, the Webmaster is a lot like an office manager. In a nutshell their job is to ensure the smooth functioning of the Website.

Most web designers are artistically inclined and are concerned mainly with with the overall design, look and feel of the website. Depending upon the size of the I.T. department, either the Web designer or a graphic artist will be responsible for creating the graphics. The Web designer on a large site will typically work closely with the Web developer. Both Web design and Web development are very specialized.

> ### HEY LOOK, IT'S A CLUE!
>
> **But I don't have an I.T. Department...**
>
> *In the case of home-based, small and medium businesses, either a third party Web design company is used or an individual Webmaster is hired. If you or your company has a modest (or non-existent) I.T. budget, then you may want to consider contracting or hiring a Webmaster. Webmasters typically have a decent understanding of both design and development.*

Typically an individual has either good design skills or programming skills. Seldom does one individual posses both. Though for smaller sites with more modest needs, a Webmaster will handle both design and development.

This leaves the Web developer. Developers are more code oriented and will be required for dynamic, e-commerce, or other Websites that are more interactive. With the demand for Web applications and a general migration to building more Websites that do more, developers are becoming highly sought after.

You may not need all of that though; in the case of home-based, small and medium businesses, either a third party Web design company is used or an individual Webmaster is hired. If you or your company has a modest (or non-existent) I.T. budget, then you may want to consider contracting or hiring a Webmaster. Webmasters typically have a decent understanding of both design and development.

If you have a small to nearly nonexistent budget, you can still compete...

There are plenty of resources available online to supplement a good Webmasters ability. If you choose a Webmaster with stronger design skills, there are plenty of scripts and modules (both free and commercially available) available to add any necessary functionality. Likewise, there are plenty of resources available for Webmasters with stronger development skills such as design templates, stock graphics and the like.

CHAPTER FIFTEEN

CHOOSING THE RIGHT WEBMASTER

*I*t never ceases to surprise me how little time some Website owners spend on their Website. This applies particularly in the case of businesses that are depending on their Website to perform. I have noticed, that a many people expect their Webmaster to develop, brand and market their website for them. This is of course including content specific to their particular business.

> ### HEY LOOK, IT'S A CLUE!
>
> **An Ounce of Preparation**
>
> If you spend a little time organizing your thoughts, preparing, and knowing what to ask you will save countless hours of frustration and your website will turn out infinitely better. This will make your job marketing it much easier.

The Internet offers small, home, and medium-sized businesses an enormous opportunity to compete with much larger companies and entities on a relatively level playing field. However, there is no free lunch and the Internet is no exception to this rule. You are likely to be facing some stiff competition. You can get to the top, but you need to be prepared, educated, patient and willing to spend some time with your Webmaster.

Large companies are undoubtedly going to pour money into their online presence and are likely to have large in-house I.T departments to maintain and support their

Website. Additionally they will have many resources for marketing it. While this gives them a good advantage, a smart Website owner has some advantages of his own.

To start with, here are some things that you should ask your potential webmaster. If you spend a little time organizing your thoughts, preparing and taking the time to write down what you want to ask him you will save countless hours of frustration and your website will turn out infinitely better. This will make your job marketing it much easier.

> **Hey Look, A Clue!**
>
> **Ch-Ch-Ch-Changes**
>
> If you don't have many changes and you expect your website to basically remain the same, then you can simply negotiate a maintenance plan with your Webmaster.
>
> However, if you do expect frequent changes, then you can do it yourself, hire an employee, or pay substantial fees.

I recommend that you make a trip to your local bookstore and pick out a nice bound blank book. They're not very expensive and because they look much nicer than a spiral notebook, there is a good chance it will survive better and be there in five years or so when you need it. However, if you would like, I have included several blank pages for you to take notes on throughout this book.

Here is a short list of questions that you can ask of your potential Webmaster. These are just suggestions, feel free to make changes, or add questions of your own as you see fit. Good luck!

- o **When will it be completed?** It is important that you get an actual date as opposed to a general timeframe like "about two weeks..." For example; March 10 is a day that you can mark on your calendar, "About two weeks" usually ends up being two more, then two more and can be end up being several months.

  Notes:

- o **What do you need from me?** Write this information down as it is being discussed. Be as detailed as possible. Take your time and be sure to get everything.

  Notes:

○ **What does that mean?** If you don't understand something or are not 100% certain that you know what your Webmaster is talking about ask for an explanation. A good Webmaster will take the time to listen to you, address your concerns, and explain everything that you don't understand.

Notes:

○ **How do I add, edit and delete content?** In many cases you will need to frequently update your website content. Depending on how your Website is set up this may or may not be easy to do.

Notes:

o **How much is this going to cost?** Find out how and when your Webmaster is going to bill. Some charge a flat fee for setup and others go with an hourly or per Diem rate. Make sure you know what you're getting into and how long/how much you'll have to pay and get it in writing.

Notes:

o **Can I have a backup copy?** Once your website is finished make sure that you get a backup copy.

Notes:

o **Where is this going to be hosted**? Make sure you know where your Website will be hosted and what the login information is. Make sure you write them down either in this book or in your permanent web notebook if you have one.

Notes:

o **Will forms and/or Web applications be included?** Lead generation and contact forms along with other interactive components are obviously a crucial part of any customer/client driven website. What you are trying to find out here is if application development is included in the quoted price.

Notes:

o **Is this a template site?**

> o **If so, how many subscribers are there?** In other words how many other Websites are out there that either look exactly like yours, or relatively similar?

Notes:

o **Does this site, or can it, use RSS feeds?** RSS stands for really simple syndication. It means that the website can gather information from various other sources on the fly. RS as gives you the opportunity to provide your visitors with up to them and a dynamic content. This keeps your website fresh and helps to ensure that your visitors come back

Notes:

o **What about e-mail?**

Notes:

How many e-mail accounts can I have?

Notes:

o **How big are they and is there a file size limit**

Notes:

o **Are there spam filters? If so, can I control them?**

Notes:

o **Can I have a mailing list**

Notes:

o **Is there a limit on the number of emails that I can send out every month?**

Notes:

o **Are there any limitations on the file types that I can accept, or send as attachments?**

Notes:

o **Are any of this hosting company's email servers blacklisted?**

Notes:

o **Do I understand this correctly?** Before you're through with the conversation take a moment to briefly go through your notes to ensure that you have all the information down properly so there's no miscommunication later on

Add whatever questions you feel necessary to this...

CHAPTER SIXTEEN

COMMUNICATING WITH YOUR WEBMASTER

ow that you've selected your Webmaster it is time to get started. For some reason, many people think that developing a Website is relatively easy thing. It's not. There is a pretty complicated process, particularly where custom Websites are concerned.

First a flowchart needs to be created detailing the different sections, pages and general navigation, and then the basic mockup of the look and feel needs to be designed. After this the domain needs to be set up and the work starts. The graphics and page structure are created. Then, the functionality and programming need to be set up and tested, followed by the addition of content. After this the Website needs to be proofread and checked for bugs, consistency and broken links. This is all much easier said than done.

You can choose to leave it all to your Webmaster to hash out. Many times this is the case. However, your Webmaster probably doesn't know your industry the way you do, nor can he speak for your services. This is why it is important to simply communicate with your Webmaster. If you are technophobic then there is really no need to worry. Chances are you will only need to provide guidance and information regarding your business and how it works. Your Webmaster should take care of all of the details.

For the best results, I strongly recommend using some form of instant messaging system. It is more responsive than email and can be extremely helpful. I personally use Microsoft Instant Messenger and been very happy with it. However, it doesn't matter if you use smoke signals and a carrier pigeon if that is what works the best for you and your Webmaster, just as long as you have a good communication system in place.

By maintaining good communication you will accomplish several things. For instance, your Website will come out more the way you envision it. Also, your content will be more accurate, your site navigation and layout will be easier to use for your customers, due to the fact that you probably know what they will be looking for much better than your Webmaster. Besides, you will learn a lot about Web design, functionality and many other things that will help you out in the future.

There really is no end to it. A good strong communication channel with your Webmaster will benefit not only your Website but also your relationship with him for years to come.

To take this is step further; often Website owners become disillusioned or disappointed with their web developer due to poor communication that ends in complete misunderstandings.

As business on the Internet continues to progress it is essential to have a good relationship with your Webmaster. If you get on the right foot early, there's virtually no limit to what you can do.

Communication is vital for success, so make certain that you talk to your Webmaster on a regular basis. Remember, nobody is going to care more about your business than you.

CHAPTER SEVENTEEN

LAYOUT AND DESIGN

If you know what you want your Website to look like or have something particular in mind; spending a few moments to simply sketch the design out on a piece of paper will help. It does not need to be pretty; nobody expects you to be Leonardo Di Vinci. However, it can really help to clarify what you have in mind.

If you are not exactly sure how you want your Website to look, or you do not have your heart set on anything particular, you may want to go with your Webmaster's best judgment. That just depends on how much the overall design matters to you.

"As long as the site is: easy to navigate, has a clear purpose, is functional and easy to use, the majority of your visitors will have a positive experience."

While the look and feel of a Website is important, it is basically a matter of taste; functionality on the other hand needs to be practical. Regardless of the look and feel of the site, the functionality must make sense. If people have to try too hard to figure out what to do, where to go, or how to get there, then there is a good chance that you will lose that visitor's business.

You should strive to make your site intuitive and easy to use. The less your visitors have to think about using the site, the more they can focus on whatever it is that you are try to tell/sell them. As long as the site is: easy to navigate, has a clear purpose, is functional and easy to use, the majority of your visitors will have a positive experience.

Think about it for a moment. When you go to a Website that has a confusing menu system, or is difficult to operate how long does it take you to get frustrated? Once frustrated your visitors will either leave, or become hostile and irate. Unless you really like dealing with irritated people, it is best to just keep it simple when it comes to navigation and functionality.

Again, don't make your visitors think! Make sure the purpose of the site is straight forward and clear. Make it simple and easy to sign up and/or buy. Give them multiple ways to get to whatever it is that they came for. Moreover, make sure it is easy to contact you. Also, provide easy to find links to all important services in logical places and make sure that no matter where someone is on your Website, they can get anywhere else within three clicks. Make it easy for your customers to give you money (or find whatever content you want them to see).

You can get a lot of inspiration from other sites that have been successful. Take a few hours to actively surf some of the major Websites that have been around for a few years. They don't have to be in your industry... Observe how they use graphics, where the navigation bar is, how many clicks does it take to get what you want. Compare them to Websites that have "taken off" and see what they have in common. Take notes on what you think makes them successful.

Register for an account. Is it easy, if so, why? Did you get frustrated? How could it have been done more elegantly? How could it have been done simpler? Take it step by step and make notes. Make a small purchase even.

If you are really daring, set up an eBay store. With all due respect eBay has a lot going on; however, I personally found it to be less than a pleasant experience. Once I got squared away I learned the nuances, but it took more time and trouble than I was happy with. In my experience, I had to spend far too much time searching for relatively straightforward things. I ran into a lot of dead ends and my impression of the whole experience was decidedly unfavorable. Don't take my word for it, try it yourself. Write down what you like and what you do not like.

On the other end of the spectrum, I have been very happy with Blogger.com. It was easy to sign up, and a snap to set up my blog. The whole thing from registering to publishing my first post only took me about fifteen minutes. I was very happy with the system and I still use it today. Everything is logically placed and easy to use. In fact, several features that I wouldn't have even thought of were so easy to use and intuitive I was able to add impressive features to my blog with a few simple clicks.

The difference in the two experiences is vast. In the case of eBay, I spent more time then I should have needed to and ended up frustrated and irritated. Whereas Blogger.com left me excited and inspired. So much so, that I could hardly wait to publish my next post. I am not trying to infer that eBay is difficult so much as it is frustrating and not intuitive to navigate. You may have a different experience.

Both way, be mindful of your visitors experience and plan accordingly. Here are a few tips, use them as you see fit, ultimately you will need to decide what works best for you:

- **What is not there matters, almost as much as what is.** The use of white space (it can be any color, not just white) helps your visitors to read your content of the Website. If your website is cluttered and has many things all vying for your visitor's attention chances are your visitor will be overwhelmed and not know where to look. Generally, when this happens your visitor simply moves on. Plenty of whitespace will give your Website a cleaner neater general appearance. *This can be a difficult task if you have a lot of information to "get out there".

- **Make sure your navigation is easy to find and use.** Nothing gets visitors to say "Let's try a different Website..." like a navigation bar that is: difficult to use, unwieldy, hard to find, or simply not what the user expects. While a kitschy navigation bar may seem clever to you, it may not be so clear to a user. This can cause your visitor to become frustrated and/or confused. A tricky navigation bar can have seriously adverse effect on your traffic. Keep in mind; while you know what you are trying to accomplish, your visitors may not be on the same wavelength. If it is difficult to get around your site many visitors will often become frustrated and leave.

- **Keep it simple.** Do not make your visitors think! Let's face it when people are surfing the web they do not want to work too hard. Take as much time as you need to intelligently design both your content and your website. It is possible that millions of people will visit your site. If it looks unprofessional, contains typographical errors or is hard to navigate, you risk frustrating people and losing the visitor/sale.

- **Errata.** Double check, triple check, quadruple check and have other people check for spelling errors, grammatical errors, broken links, inconsistent formatting and factual errors. Afterwards, check again. The last thing you want is for your potential clients/customers to visit your website and notice errors. To put it mildly, this makes you look incompetent; if you can even spell why should they trust you buy new product or service?

- **Uniformity.** The pages within your Website should have the same basic look and feel. This also pertains to the navigation system. Unless you have a very good reason to do so, try to keep the each page design and structure exactly the same as other pages in the site. This will help create a uniform look and feel throughout the site that will tie it all together. When a visitor comes to a website they expect to see this. It makes it simpler for people to get around within the site and it makes it easier for them to understand.

- **Clarity.** Try to be as clear and concise in both your design and your content. The average Website visitor will spend only moments on your website to determine whether they are going to look at it in more depth are not. Think about your own habits. If you search for "health insurance" millions of sites will come up. Your choices are virtually limitless. It is a matter of one mouse click to look at each site. I don't know about you, but a Website has only seconds to impress me one way or the other. This is why it's important to have an appealing site that gets your message across immediately.

- **Color and aesthetics**. Colors have always been challenging for me personally. I have in some cases, spending hours laboring over color schemes. I recommend that you choose a color scheme and stick with it. If you tell your webmaster that you don't care about colors (as many of my clients have) then you don't have a lot of ground to complain if you don't like what he comes up with. If that's the case, fine, but be prepared to pay extra if you want to make changes after word. Fortunately, I have listed some tools and utilities that can help you nail down a color scheme that you want to use. Just visit my website www.EverMoreTech.com and go to the design tips section.

- **Graphics and images**. Your graphics and images should be the highest quality possible. This is essential; professional images will provide your visitors with a positive initial impression of your website and typically make the site more readable in general.

There are many Websites that offer reasonably priced images. I have included a list of resources at www.EverMoreTech.com I encourage you to take a look. Good stock photography can be either very hard to find or extremely expensive.

- **Browsers & platforms.** Before you give your Webmaster your final blessing on the design, make sure to look at it in several different browsers and resolutions. You will need to make sure your website looks and works as desired in different browsers, screen resolutions and platforms.

Take some time with this. In the long run you be very glad you did. If you spend some time intelligently planning how your Website will look and feel, as well as, how users will interact and find information; you will never regret it. Remember, the more you think the less your visitors will have to.

CHAPTER EIGHTEEN

GRAPHICS AND LOGOS

*A*s a Web developer, one of the most difficult things that I face when designing a new Website is that first blank page. Sometimes, inspiration strikes early on and it's not much of a problem, In that case, I can quite easily whip up a quick masthead complete with embedded logo. Other times I can look at that same blank page for days and nothing... When a client comes with a logo already designed (assuming that it's a quality piece) then a large part of troublesome work is already done.

> ### Note a Quote
>
> *"When a client comes with a logo already designed (assuming that it's a quality piece) then a large part of troublesome work is already done."*

Depending upon how artistic you are; you may, or may not, be able to do your own logo. If you are not up to the task don't worry, either have your Webmaster handle it, or have a professional logo service design a custom logo to your specifications. Just remember if you decide to go with your Webmaster you'll probably save a few bucks, but his job is to develop Websites rather than graphic art. While there is quite a bit of overlap and many web designers and developers are fairly handy with graphics programs, a professional graphic artist that specializes in logo design may be desirable depending on your budget.

113

Of course this all depends on the skill and ability of the Webmaster you are working with.

Once you've decided on a logo you should take a few moments to think about how you want the overall look and feel of your Website to be. Feel free to make sketches or any notes you believe will be helpful. There are several different elements which you will need to think about. It is also a good idea to have some photos and graphics ready for your Webmaster. If you visit www.EverMoreTech.com and click Webmaster tools you will find links to graphics and stock photography Websites. Many of the images only cost a dollar or two and can save you hundreds of dollars.

CHAPTER NINETEEN

ANOTHER HELPING OF HTML

opefully, by now you've had the time to let the previous chapter regarding basic HTML sink in. Now it is time to take a closer look at the hypertext markup language. Specifically; we will take a look at tags that help to create page structure and layout. Finally, we will explore what cascading style sheets are and how various other elements are used.

Let's start with basic page structure and layout.

> **Note a Quote**
>
> *"Remember, it is not necessary to know HTML, but a basic understanding can be helpful in the long run. If it confuses you or you are not interested in learning, then it is ok to skip past this chapter and continue to the rest of the book."*

A basic Website, built purely in HTML will typically use tables to create page structure (most modern sites use Cascading Style Sheets and other technologies in addition to "plain old" HTML, but we will stick to basic HTML to better illustrate how this all works). A table is simply a grid of rows and columns forming boxes. Each box, known as a "**cell**", can contain graphics and or text (content). Furthermore a cell can contain additional tables.

The practice of putting a table within a table is known as nesting tables. This can all be a bit confusing until you get the hang of it. If you are familiar with spreadsheets there are some similarities. For instance;

This is "Table A". This is Cell 1 of Table A.	This is Cell 2 of Table A.
This is Cell 3 of Table A; it contains another table (Table B). This is Table B, Cell 1 Table B, Cell 2 Table B, Cell 3 This is still Cell 3 of Table A, It encapsulates Table B. Table B is a known as a nested table.	This is Cell 4 of Table A.

While it is not the most elegant solution, it provides a basic way to structure HTML. this is the basis of most basic HTML websites. In some cases, rows or columns can be merged into one larger sell that Spans two or more rows or columns. By simply spanning the first row across the second column we will have a very basic website structure. See the diagram below:

Masthead (Table A –Row 1 Column 1 & 2 merged)	
Navigation column (Table A –Row 2 Column 1)	**Content** (Table A –Row 2 Column 1)

Within the Navigation column:

Navigation button one (Table B –Row 2 Column 1)
Navigation button two (Table B –Row 2 Column 1)
Navigation button three (Table B –Row 2 Column 1)

Navigation column
(Table A –Row 2 Column 1)
Continued

Additional information that you would like to set apart from the main body of content would go here. This would include: advertising information, special announcements and general knickknacks.

A little color, a few graphics, and there you have it; a very basic brochure type website.

Acme Fine Jewelry & Rockets

A Ridiculous

Fictitious Company!

- Home
- **Gold & Silver**
- **Pearls & Gemstones**
- **Solid Fuel Rockets**
- **Booster Rockets**
- **About Us**
- **Contact**

Welcome to Acme Fine Jewelry & Rockets!

At Acme, you will only find the very best Jewelry and Rockets available. So whether you are looking for earrings for that Special Someone, or need a reliable launch vehicle for your newest communications satellite, we are your one stop shop for the hottest designs!

Just one look at our catalog and we think you will agree, Acme is the top!

Hurry! Act quickly and you will get your choice of a free rhinestone pendant, or a selenium pu36 explosive space modulator with every purchase of an X-10 re-entry vehicle! * Offer good while supplies last!

Once you have the basic concepts and syntax down, the rest is just a matter of design and making it all work. This is of course with the exception of any scripting, but you get the idea...

We will look at the different markup and tags later on in this chapter. I would even include some code to make a basic website. If you take a look at appendix b, you will find some very basic code for simple complete website similar to the one above.

If you are feeling ambitious and think you can do this on your own, or your budget dictates that you will do this on your own regardless, it might be a good place for you to start. With that said, I will reiterate ; this book is not meant to teach you web design, however, if you are able to pick up the ball and run with it, then by all means, go for it.

Just remember: if you sit down to design a web page, make certain there's nothing else you'll have to do for really long time. Time loses its meaning once you start developing a web page. Chances are you'll sit down intending to spend half an hour, maybe even a couple of hours working on your site on a nice Saturday afternoon. Before you know it, it's Tuesday, and you've grown a beard. Yes, unfortunately, in some cases this applies to the ladies as well...

Of course the Website template above is somewhat rudimentary. It is done with pure HTML. This approach to web design is relatively easy in straightforward. However, it has been devalued in favor of more capable technologies such as: cascading style sheets (CSS), Extensible Markup Language (XML), ASP.NET and many others. Outside of a brief overview of CSS, I will not get into any detail regarding other languages.

This brings us to Cascading Style Sheets. CSS allows you to modify existing HTML tags or create completely new styles by attaching style definitions either contained in a separate file and linking to it or directly in the head section of the page that will use them. These styles can modify HTML tags or be used to create classes.

The styles are overlaid on top of one another in the same manner overhead transparencies can be. CSS styles affect how the tag is rendered.

Note a Quote

"Time loses its meaning once you start developing a web page. Chances are you'll sit down intending to spend half an hour, maybe even a couple of hours working on your site on a nice Saturday afternoon. Before you know it, it's Tuesday, and you've grown a beard."

For clarity; if you remember the builder and blueprint analogy I used to describe how browsers work, than it will be easier to understand. CSS gives our imaginary architect the ability to use a legend to change/add/edit the different symbols used to create the blueprint. In other words, by using CSS, a designer can make the "<b>"tag (the bold tag) do more than simply bold the enclosed text. He could format the text not only is bold, but also in red and at a different size. All he would need to do is include the style in the style sheet attached to a web page (or in the head section of the page itself).

I'm not going to get into CSS in any depth other than what I've just told you. This is just a primer designed simply so you'll know what your webmaster is talking about if it should come up in your discussions. If you are interested in learning more about CSS or its uses, there are many books out there, or you can stop by the discussion forums at EvermoreTech.com and post any questions you may have.

Now that I have thrown another term at you, I should probably let you know that there is a glossary of terms that will help explain what these terms are and what they mean. Considering the nature of technology, there are new terms being used all the time. To help you deal with this, at www.EverMoreTech.com I have a "living glossary" of terms that I will keep updated over time.

CHAPTER TWENTY

SCREEN RESOLUTION

*V*ery simply put, screen resolution is the number of dots that you see on your screen. The screen resolution determines how much virtual "real estate" you have to work with on your monitor.

In other words; if two computers were side by side and both had identical nineteen inch monitors but one computer (Computer A) was set to display 1440 by 1024 screen resolution and the other one (Computer B) was set to display a 800 by 600 screen resolution, Computer A would display more "stuff", but it would be smaller.

To elaborate; with the lower resolution objects will appear larger with a higher resolution objects will appear smaller but you'll have more space to work with. A good analogy is a convex rearview mirror. You know the ones I'm talking about that little stamp impression that says things are larger than the scene and they give you a larger field of view same sort of thing with the screen resolution your objects are smaller but you have more area to work with.

To illustrate exactly what this means take a look at the screen shots.

A screenshot of my desktop viewed at 1440 x 900

A screenshot of my desktop viewed at 800 x 600

Along with cross browser and cross platform compatibility screen resolution comprises one of the things you need to look out for if your website is too wide that it will make your visitors to have smaller monitors or larger monitors with lower resolution do a lot of horizontal scrolling in. The majority of users find it exceeded only a retaining and you should try to work with your web developer to either come up with a dynamic design that will alter its width to fit the screen size and resolution of the visitor or use a fixed width that will be viewable in an 800 by 600 pixel screen resolution size.

CHAPTER TWENTY-ONE

ADA COMPLIANCE

The American disability act was designed to help those amongst us with physical challenges. You may not know it, but there are many things on either a Macintosh or a PC to assist people with disabilities. These range from high contrast collar schemes to speech assisted computing. In fact, when I was going to school (yes they had computers then) to become Microsoft certified, one of my classmates was completely blind. He had an application that would audibly tell him what his mouse cursor was hovering over. What computers can do for people that face challenges every day is remarkable.

As a website owner it is important to tell your webmaster that you want to ensure that your website is ADA compliant and easily accessible by all users. Your Webmaster should already know this, but it is a good thing to make it a point.

CHAPTER TWENTY-TWO

DIFFERENT TYPES OF WEBSITES

STATIC WEBSITES

Static Websites also known as Brochure Websites are Websites that don't change often. The content remains the same, the navigation remains the same, and the overall presentation remains the same for all users. In most cases there is little interactivity outside of the standard buttons.

Static Websites can be updated manually. However the majority of Website owners that run static Websites seldom if ever update them. Often a Website owner will commission a Webmaster to develop the Website. However, once completed the Webmaster, typically interested in mundane things like... eating... is forced to move on and work other projects. So unless the business is willing to either: enter into a service contract, do the changes "in-house" or pay the Webmaster for changes, the site remains as is.

In many cases, this is absolutely fine. In many others, it is not and the website will either need maintenance or it will become outdated.

DYNAMIC WEBSITES

*A*s the name suggests a dynamic Website is one that changes often. It may change every time a particular user logs in, or perhaps when new products or information becomes available. Whatever the case, there are many different technologies and approaches that can be employed to create a

> ### HEY LOOK, IT'S A CLUE!
>
> **Just The Facts Ma'am**
>
> Your job (fortunately) is not to know the all the technical aspects other of your Website other than the basics that you will need to know to administrate it.

dynamic Website. Some of the solutions commonly used are: Database Driven Sites, XHTML, XML, RSS, PERL, and ASP.NET along with many others and of course, new solutions are being innovated constantly. I realize that you may not know what all of this means. Fortunately you do not to know the all the technical aspects and details of your Website. All you need to know are the basic things that you will need to administrate it.

Therefore, to simplify things, a dynamic Website derives some or all of its content from a data source. That data source is easy to manipulate. In other words it is simple to add, edit, or delete information to and from the data source by either yourself, an external force (info drawn from another source such as an external system or Website), or the Website visitors themselves.

In most cases, administering a dynamic Website is relatively simple: Typically there is some sort of control panel or similar tool that allows administrators to add and change information on the site. If you have a little bit of patience they are generally easy to master after a couple hours of tinkering.

Patience is the key. I have observed many Website owners become frustrated when updating or adding their content. Not only is this irritating at the moment, often, the impatient Website owner will become discouraged and cease to even attempt to update the site. Of course the site inevitably withers away over time and becomes a cobweb.

If you want your visitors to return you have to keep things fresh. And the only way you that is by updating the content. If you cannot update the content yourself then you must hire somebody to do it for you. Don't think that your monthly hosting package will cover the cost of maintenance as well. Trust me on this one I personally run my own web servers and I can tell you that it's quite expensive to maintain and secure them in addition to the electric consumption and my bandwidth costs. Add to that the additional costs for the various upgrades and appropriate software will be required to make it all work. Occasionally I will have a good client that has been with me for a long time that needs some minor changes and I may make an exception.

FLASH™ WEBSITES

A Flash™ Website is a site that is based on Adobe Flash™ which is a technology that allows animation and other dynamic effect to be streamed across the Web. Because video and other animation techniques are so resource intensive, they are seldom used, or only used by companies with very deep pockets. Flash changes all of that. Flash uses client side plug-ins that enables the user's machine to do some of the work. This allows the file sizes to be smaller and thereby allows animation and other cutting edge effects and interactivity to be used much more effectively.

So your choices are relatively simple:

First you can pay your webmaster on an hourly basis for every change you want to make. I believe that this is the most expensive option, but that depends on how many changes you anticipate.

Second, you could enter into a maintenance agreement above and beyond the cost of simply hosting your website in which you're guaranteed a certain amount of time that your webmaster will agree to make changes in alterations your website. This is not a bad option if you don't want to worry about it later on and simply just want someone to do it for you. This option, I would recommend for busy people that don't have time to do it themselves. Even so, I do think that it's important that you know how to make these changes are self.

Third you can learn HTML, CSS, XML, XHTML and whatever additional technologies you will need to know to update the website yourself. Besides learning all of those technologies (and believe me we're talking about a pretty steep learning curve) you also need to buy whatever web development tools you will need, or hand code everything in a text editor. I'd don't recommend this option fleshes out with needing to know about FTP now the website files and center and so forth

Fourth you can have a dynamic Website with a control panel that you can access with a browser and make changes that way. This is my recommendation for most people. Quite frankly, it offers a comprehensive solution and is a relatively easy way to add or modify content. Depending upon the dynamic solution that you choose it may be considered a content management system for CMS.

There are a few different content management systems out there today. Some notable ones, at the time of this writing, are Microsoft's SharePoint services, DotNetNuke, and PHPNuke. Although there are many more these seem to be the most popular at this time. While the exact name or type of Framework is probably pretty unimportant. I mentioned these simply because they have a large community support group by high in them. If your site is built on one of the preceding platforms than there is a good chance that you'll be able to find modules that will do what you want them to do for free, or at little charge. I will provide more information about framework websites later on.

CHAPTER TWENTY-THREE

W3C COMPLIANCE

The W3C is the organization that develops standards for the web. In other words, the W3C are the people that determine the rules regarding HTML, CSS and whatever other language a webmaster might use. W3C stands for World Wide Web Consortium. It determines how browsers should behave and how they should interpret code.

Without these rules it would be pandemonium on the web. If there were no standards, websites would be written in a hodgepodge of different languages and nothing would be compatible from one browser to the next. Imagine for a moment that there were no traffic laws. You can imagine what trouble that would be.

Despite the fact that the standards are so important not all browsers adhere to them. In fact, Microsoft's Internet Explorer is one of these so called rogue browsers. Microsoft has included some HTML tags that other browsers do not support. They also interpret some HTML tags a little differently than W3C compliant browsers. Because Internet explorer has such dominance amongst browsers they can get away with this.

Despite the fact that it's nice to have extra functionality, it makes it very difficult to develop a website that is functional and displays properly in all browsers.

It is up to your webmaster to ensure that your website is W3C compliant. There are many tools that you can use to help you make sure that your site is compliant. You can visit EverMoreTech.com for a list of my favorites

Remember, it's not your job to fix any mistakes you may find. All you have to do is simply point them out to your webmaster. I it is extremely important to go through every single page of your website to check for various errors including; grammar and typos, broken links, images that display incorrectly in addition to any problems caused by viewing your web page in different browsers.

CHAPTER TWENTY-FOUR

FORMS, SCRIPTS & LANGUAGES

Here is where the rubber meets the road for dynamic sites. This chapter deals with many complicated technical concepts. I am including this chapter for those of you, who are technically advanced, or desire an in-depth understanding of how dynamic websites work.

The typical website owner does not need to know much about writing programming code other than the basic concepts involved. However, understanding the basics can help with the creation and maintenance of your website. It is a good idea to know basically what is going on so you will be able to make intelligent choices.

If you have no interest in the nitty gritty details of how websites work then feel free to skip this chapter. However, if you believe you'll be taking an active role creating and or maintaining your website then read on.

Basically, there are two distinct aspects of programming:

1. **Syntax** – this is the actual code itself. It consists of all the stuff that the programmer writes. It is the actual nuts and bolts of the program or website.

2. **Logic** – this is the actual thinking behind the code. In other words, this is the logical steps used to

determine how to actually write the code. This is the real magic behind the program. You will never see it on the written page, but it exists in the flow charts and all the planning that was put together before the first line of code was ever written.

FORMS

This is one of the most basic uses of simple programming. Most likely your website will include one or more forms. A form is simply an interactive element that allows a website visitor to send information back to the server where is processed accordingly. The server can do a number of things with this information such as; save it to a database, send an email, redirect the user to a different page, or display information, all based on the information submitted.

> ### Note a Quote
>
> *"While you can always add more forms later it is best to be as thorough as possible up front. Sometimes simple changes can require enormous rewrites to the code. Therefore, the more complete and well thought out the initial plan and design is, the smoother the design process will be while producing better results."*

Additionally the results collected by the use of forms will allow you to use that information in several ways. If the information that you collect from a form is stored into a database then you can retrieve that information for future use.

Forms are a very powerful tool that can be is in a number of ways and are an essential part of most web sites. You can use them to gather information about your visitors, create a mailing list and take orders, present information based on a response and an endless variety of other things.

Beyond using the data, forms also give you many new options to display data. You can personalize the users experience on your website by including their name and whatever information is appropriate. You can display results of surveys and polls directly on your website. These results are up to the minute because it is available in real time as it is added to the database. There is no end to it. The only limitation is really your imagination.

Whatever the case the information submitted will need to be processed. That means programming code. The code written for a simple form is usually pretty basic. Most generic forms can use code that has already been written. In many cases, certain framework websites or web development programs automatically write code that will handle basic forms. Depending upon the complexity of the tasks the form needs to accomplish the code can get complicated quickly.

The first thing that needs to be done is to determine exactly what the purpose of the form is, what it needs to do and how that will be accomplished. This is the logic that I was speaking of earlier. This is typically done using a flowchart. The more planning the goes into it, the easier it is to write the code and better it typically comes out

It is a good idea to take some time to consider what forms you may need to include in your website. This will simplify the design process and enable you to give your webmaster a clear idea of what you will need. You will first need to consider the basic purpose of your website. Then you will need to determine what information you will need to collect from your visitors to accomplish this. Then it is up to you and/or your webmaster to create the logic and syntax to make it happen.

While you can always add more forms later it is best to be as thorough as possible up front. Sometimes simple changes can require enormous rewrites to the code. Therefore, the more complete and well thought out the initial plan and design is, the smoother the design process will be while producing better results.

SCRIPTS & SCRIPTING

Obviously forms are different from a regular page. Forms actually do something. They allow the user to input information and then which is submitted to the server where it is processed and dealt with appropriately. That means that a script is involved. A script is a small snippet of programming code.

There are many different types of scripts and corresponding web pages. This is important for you to know because if you ever need to change web hosts you will need to know what language(s) your website uses and make sure that your new web host will support it.

Most notably are:

- ASP, ASP.net
- PHP
- Python
- Java
- JavaScript VBScript and many other "light" scripting languages.

This is just a short list and there are many others. ASP.net, JavaScript, Python and PHP are the most common. Of course this may change as time goes on. Currently, Ajax is becoming increasingly popular. No matter what language your website is written in the logic is logic and transcends whatever programming language was used.

When you are choosing a web host it is crucial to select one that supports all of the various languages that your website uses. If your web host does not support all the appropriate languages your website will crash. If you purchase a web hosting package before choosing a webmaster makes certain he can write in one of the supported languages. If you select your webmaster before your hosting package, your webmaster can probably help you choose a web host.

Typically, where there's smoke there's fire. And in the case of websites; where there are forms and/or scripting then there's usually a database somewhere. Not only does the web hosting package you select need to support the proper languages; it also must support the type of database necessary. Of course this is all discussed in the choosing a web host chapter.

If you want to know more about scripting and programming languages there are plenty of books out there that can help you. Feel free to visit www.EverMoreTech.com/books.

CHAPTER TWENTY-FIVE

FRAMEWORK WEBSITES

I briefly mentioned framework based websites earlier. Framework based websites sometimes known as Content Management Systems (CMS) and Platform Based websites warrant further explanation. Framework & Platform based websites are an excellent solution for people or companies that need to update

> ### Note a Quote
>
> "A good content management system should take only a few hours to learn but may take much longer to master."

their websites content quickly, effectively and regularly. While strictly speaking there is a difference between the two types of websites for our purposes here, I am going to refer to a customizable website based on an underlying structure as a Framework.

OK, so now let me put this into English. A framework website or a content management system is a highly functional website that can be easily adapted to suit just about any needs. Think if it as the framework of a building. It provides the basic structure a website needs.

When your web hosts gets it it's pretty plain, and then he configures it as he sees fit. When you contract with him to get a website, he goes into his portal and creates another portal for you. Depending on what you want this could be a framework that is based on a template. Even though it's based on a template it's far different than a template website. This is because everything is modular. Your web developer and then had or remove modules from your website (known to us techies as a solution). Additionally he can apply what is known as the skin, or theme. So the content modules will control what your website does and the scan will control how it looks.

Depending on your needs and your budget you can either manage the website yourself, or have your webmaster do it for you. Now, I want to be very clear. If you decide to manager content on your own even though you may save some money expected put in some major time. When you sit down to the computer to work on your website time has a way of completely vanishing I cannot stress this enough. Even though editing your content on a content management system is relatively easy, there is still a learning curve. Don't expect to sit down to your desk start hammering away at your keyboard, and end up with a Picasso. It just doesn't work that way. You'll have to first learn the program how to edit it, how everything works, and then you can get to work. I recommend that you keep this book close by and because of basic knowledge of HTML will be extremely helpful. As long as you approach it with the right attitude and expectations you can work wonders.

There are additional benefits to using a content management system. If you update your content frequently you will rank much higher in the search engines. I won't get into the technical details except to say that the frequently updated content requires search engines to index your website more often that may increase your page rank. Beyond that, with regularly updated content you stand a better chance that your visitors will keep returning.

Framework based websites are relatively straightforward and simple to use. Of course, there is no free lunch and there is a certain learning curve. However, if you have chosen a good system it will be relatively easy to learn so you can get started quickly, but comprehensive enough to handle all of your needs. In other words a good content management system should take only a few hours to learn and years to master. Additionally, a good CMS will have an active community supporting it.

The main purpose of a framework based content management system is to allow website administrators and users to maintain and update content via web browser. These websites offer a great amount of power and flexibility. The ability to update content can be determined on an individual or group basis depending on the actual user.

To clarify this; individual users or groups of users can be assigned various rights and based on what permissions are granted to their login (or lack of being logged in). For example; a user named Sam finds your website on a search engine. Sam can all only see the information that on authenticated visitors are allowed to see. By contrast when you visit the site and login additional information, pages and options are available to you.

The ability to assign rights allows you to have access to sensitive areas of your website. Therefore, you can access and administrative pages that allow you to control and manipulate the website securely. Furthermore, you

145

can allow all individual users or groups of users to have special privileges or access to premium content or information once they have logged in to the website.

As a website owner, this gives you an enormous amount of latitude, flexibility and control over your website. By simply logging in you will have authenticated yourself and your Website will "know" who you are. It will then assign your rights accordingly

You can control virtually your entire website through a simple web browser. You can add, edit or delete; content, modules, users and pages easily and quickly without programming or any expensive specialized software.

Most framework based websites will have several modules and themes included. In most cases additional modules and themes can be obtained online commercially or in some cases completely free. Depending upon the CMS that you choose and how active the community is there may be literally thousands of modules to choose from.

For a list of framework systems that I recommend visit www.EverMoreTech.com/Framework.

To reiterate; I strongly urge you to consider this type of website. This is particularly true if you plan to update the content with any kind of regularity. This can make the difference between a success and failure of your website.

A surprising number of websites fail simply because the content cannot be updated. Prices change, information becomes obsolete or outdated, images begin to get stale and products and services often change over time. If your website does not change to reflect Real-life changes then its relevance will decrease.

By contrast, a well maintained website that is updated regularly has a better than average chance of success. If you can make these changes quickly and easily without the need to depend on someone else then you are way ahead of the game. By learning how to use a framework type website you will decrease your dependence on your webmaster and the less you have to depend on the webmaster the more time and money you will save.

Here are a few things to consider when you are in the early stages of your project.

- Work with a reputable webmaster. Your webmaster doesn't have to be local; the nature of web development facilitates doing a website remotely. However, it is imperative that you have good communication with your web master. Cultivate a relationship and make sure he returns your phone calls before you start.

- Have a concrete finish date. Make sure that it's an actual date; not an arbitrary number like two weeks, but rather, March 15 (assuming that is two weeks).

- Make sure that you can easily add and edit content and make sure you know how.

- If you intend to have your webmaster update and maintain your content, make sure that you work this out in advance and get it in writing.

CHAPTER TWENTY-SIX

PROFESSIONAL GRAPHICS & PHOTOS

This can be a real challenge for many website owners. Even if you are a professional photographer, and have fairly decent skills and creating computer graphics, it will soon became apparent that you are not going to be able to take all the photographs you may need.

While various collections of photos and graphics exist, the quality and price varies drastically. A disk containing less than 100 high resolution photographs can typically cost hundreds of dollars. In other cases; the images and graphics are cheap, tacky and unusable. Even worse, it is very likely that you can spend hours searching for particular image and find nothing suitable for your needs.

This is a significant problem for many site owners. A good webmaster should have many resources available, but of course there are no guarantees. Fortunately there are many great websites that contain millions of stock photos available to the public for commercial use for just a few dollars.

If you visit www.EverMoreTech.com/WebStock I have a list of some of the stock photography websites that I like to use. Additionally, there it is a small selection of free stock images that you may use at no charge.

CHAPTER TWENTY-SEVEN

MAINTENANCE

$\mathcal{R}$egardless of the type of website package that you choose it is bound to need maintenance from time to time. If you have signed up for a do it yourself template site or you plan to use a readymade or turnkey web site that has been provided to you as part of a web hosting package, that maintenance is undoubtedly going to be up to you.

This is obviously the most low cost method. However, in the vast majority of cases, saving a few bucks can cost you the long run. Generally, it is a better idea to spend a little more time, money and effort to achieve a professional result. Consider the simple fact that your website represents your professional image online and in some cases may be the only thing that your potential customer sees. Therefore, it is of paramount importance to present the most professional looking website possible.

If you are using a professional Webmaster then you will likely have some choices regarding maintenance. Most webmasters will offer a maintenance contract with a relatively low monthly fee. In this arrangement your webmaster typically agrees to make changes when necessary. Depending on your budget, your webmasters rates, and his responsiveness this may be an excellent option.

If you do choose to enter into a maintenance agreement there are few things that you should make sure of before you commit to anything:

- Be certain that you completely understand the terms and you have the plan in writing

- Make sure your service/maintenance contract spells out exactly how much time the webmaster has to make changes and what happens if he fails to make them in a timely manner

- Be sure to check if there's a minimum/maximum amount of hours included in the contract

- Be very clear regarding the size, complexity, and frequency of changes covered under the maintenance agreement.

- Make sure that you can get out of the contract if you are dissatisfied with the service.

In lieu of a monthly maintenance contract you may choose to pay hourly or flat rate per job for whatever upkeep you may need. This route may make a lot of sense if you do not need to change your content often, or it can be quite pricey if you do have substantial changes regularly.

Keep in mind that many people underestimate the time is going to take the webmaster to make a "simple" change. For instance; sometimes changing a literally takes under five minutes. However, there are cases when "simply" changing a link or some text is a major ordeal. This is particularly true on flash websites or other Websites that are less flexible than your average standard Website such as a dynamic website where the link is a result of some sort of function.

The inverse is also true; many people overestimate the amount of time it takes to make certain changes and therefore are open to getting ripped off. Hopefully your webmaster is a relatively honest person, but that is something you will have to decide for yourself.

If you have a good content management system you can usually enjoy the best of both worlds. You can keep your maintenance costs down because the website will be much easier to administrate. This is of course due to the fact that you can change most of the content yourself.

This is different from a basic template site. Even though you can also change the content yourself, the framework based site is much more dynamic, flexible and less like a cookie cutter website. Additionally, most framework sites boast new features and functionality that regularly become available. Most framework websites are either open source or provide APIs so your web developer can create custom modules based on your exact needs

So you see framework based websites offer a great deal of power and flexibility that can grow and change with your needs.

For more information regarding framework sites and links to several free systems you can visit my website www.EverMoreTech.com/CMS

CHAPTER TWENTY-EIGHT

EXPECTATIONS

*I*ronically, one of the hidden pitfalls that really cause problems; the owner's overly optimistic expectations. This is something that you should definitely be aware of. If you want to simply build a website and expect that website to turn a huge profit the first month... You are likely to be disappointed. While it is possible for a Website to be a smash hit right out of the chute, it is not usually the case. Invariably it takes a bucket of money or an enormous amount of work for such a thing to happen. Typically when a website is launched nobody even knows it's there.

Think of your website as in if it were an island rising out of the middle of the Pacific Ocean. When you first launch it, it is just another uncharted island amongst thousands. It is up to you to make sure that your website is discovered and once discovered is attractive or useful enough to encourage people to visit. Only then can you consider your website a success.

Allow me to clarify. When you build and launch your site, nobody will know it is there. First, the website must be optimized and submitted to the major search engines. This will put it on the map and help your perspective visitors find it. Then unless you are extremely lucky and benefit from some sort of user driven viral marketing, you will need to run some sort of marketing campaign yourself. There are many different options available to you that we will explore in depth later on in the book. Then depending upon what type of sites you were running, with a little luck you will begin to build a community of users that can help build your traffic from a trickle into a flood.

The key to all of this is to be realistic, tenacious and patient.   If you have realistic expectations and put some effort into the creation   upkeep   and

> ### Note a Quote
>
> *""if you think you can, or if you think you can't, you're right.." –Henry Ford*

marketing of your website, over time you stand an excellent chance of being rewarded with steadily increasing flow of traffic visiting your site. It is actually quite straightforward. Build a good site, make sure that is loaded with useful content or products and market the heck out of it and lastly, be sure to provide your visitors with excellent customer service.

All too often the owner of an outstanding new website has expectations that are unrealistic become frustrated, lose interest and abandon the Website.   Unrealistic expectations have the tendency to give the impression that little or no work will be required to make the website successful. This just isn't the case, realistically; it will take a lot of hard work, time, money and patience to do it properly.

Make sure that you're willing to invest the proper resources into your website project. This doesn't mean that it is going to take a boatload of cash, mounds of work or heaps of precious time all at once. Certainly, if all of these things are available to you in abundance so much the better, then you can watch your site in a flurry of fanfare.

While it does take considerable effort, time and money they are proportional. Being proportional to one another means that they can be substituted to a certain degree for one another; for instance if you have more time than money, you can do spend more time promoting your site using various guerrilla tactics that are often free. If you have more money than time than more conventional types of advertising such as pay per click or a widespread banner campaign may make more sense for you.

By simply having realistic expectations from the start you will be much better prepared to do what is necessary to ensure the success of your site. As time progresses hopefully you will find that there is good in concrete reason to be optimistic. If you accept that even with hard work and a lot of money it's going to take it least four to six months or even longer to see real traffic on your site, then hunker down and do the work, every day that goes by you can watch your statistics increase... If you keep it up, your stats are likely to continue increasing until your website reaches a "critical mass" where it will basically sustain itself and further marketing is just more fuel for the fire.

It is just logical. All of the things described in this chapter are the essential ingredients needed to build a great website. Assuming you have a great website that provides something that people want... well the cream always floats to the top doesn't it? The same idea applies online.

The Internet is the great equalizer. A very small company can have a very large web presence in compete with the monolithic multinational conglomerates on equal footing. In fact a small company arguably has the advantage of being nimble. Never before in history has it been so easy to compete at this level. This is probably why so many people make the mistake of thinking "if you build it they will come." In reality, it's more like "if you build it, work really hard at it, then market the heck out of it, and have something that people want, and then maybe... they might come."

CHAPTER TWENTY-NINE

SEARCH ENGINE OPTIMIZATION A.K.A. SEO

Obviously, your ultimate goal should be to get a high ranking with Google™ and other major search engines. Getting a high ranking for a major keyword on one of the top search engines is like hitting a grand slam home run that wins the World Series. Snagging a choice keyword virtually guarantees sky high traffic. For a popular keyword hundreds of thousands or even millions of users can be directed to your website *hourly*.

Of course, getting a top listing on a prime keyword is much easier said than done. Depending upon what your website is about you may or may not be facing stiff competition. For instance if you are real estate agent in a major metropolitan area and you have a website, a quick search for *"Los Angeles Real Estate"* on Google returns 1,840,000 results.

Considering that by default Google returns ten results per page, and website with an average page ranking would show up somewhere around page 92,000 (1,840,000 divided by ten = 184,000 then divide that by half end up on page 92,000). I don't know about you, but I don't find myself looking through 92,000 pages of search results very often... besides, Google limits the number of websites that it will actually display.

159

Regular listings (not paid advertisements), known as **organic listings** are the Rosetta stone to generating massive traffic. As I said above competition is fierce for popular keywords.

So what should you do? You can probably start with the obvious answer; make sure your site is better than most of the other sites out there. In fact, reach for the Brass ring, try and make it the best web site. This alone should give you an excellent advantage over your competition. Additionally, search engines can only read text; they cannot "read" images. Therefore, if you don't have good text content on your website then you face a serious challenge as far as search engine ranking is concerned.

Additionally, you will generally achieve better results if you target specific keywords. If you focus on a niche and write your content so that includes words that are focused on a specific skill, aspect or location of whatever it is that you are offering you stand a better chance of being found on a search engine. For example; if you own a shop that fixes automotive air conditioning units, make sure that you point that out. Air conditioning is such a broad search term that it's likely that you'll get buried in the search results. However, if you have your website optimized for in each search term you will have better luck. In this case, *Torrance automotive air conditioning service* gives you an excellent chance of being found on the first few pages.

Next, make sure your website is formatted properly. It will help your website ranking if it is formatted well. Headings, italicized words, bold text, and alt tags can have a tremendous impact on your websites rankings when used properly. Similarly, avoid broken links and pages that say "under construction".

There are many more ways to increase your ranking. Work to increase your link popularity, add fresh content regularly, start a blog, become the active in community forums and write press releases.

There is much to know about search engine optimization. If you're truly serious about getting traffic and this is an area that you should study on an ongoing basis. Search engine optimization is one of the most important factors to a website success. While I can provide you with a good foundation of understanding SEO is a large and in-depth topic that is changing and evolving every day. If you visit my website at www.EverMoreTech.com/SEO, you will find more information and some recommended tools, links and reading material that can help you get the most out of your website.

Below is a list of the fundamental things that you should consider doing to ensure favorable search engine ranking. Please bear in mind that this is by no means a definitive list and many of the techniques discussed your will be elaborated on in further chapters.

- **Build a good website** –Google itself states: the best way to ensure good search results is to design a good site that people want to see. Google further cautions against developing your website specifically with site rankings in mind. In other words, design your site for people and write content that is easy to read and informational and your site should do relatively well.

Even though that is extremely good practice, it is wise to cover all your bases and employ some fundamental SEO techniques in addition. Keep reading for a description of what these are.

- **Target specific key words** –by being more specific with keywords and targeting a local area or some other niche market will help you stand out from the crowd. If you work toward attracting visitors that are local or are looking for something specific than your chances of achieving a high ranking increase. Not only will you increase your chances of being found by a niche market, you will still be in the running for the broader search terms. For example; if you optimize your website for the keywords "Manhattan pet supply, and food specializing in exotic fish" not only will your localized and niche markets of Manhattan exotic fish return results, the broader search terms of pet supply and food and any combination of these keywords will all return results. This effectively maximizes your potential to attract visitors.

- **Avoid broken links and poor formatting** –broken links, missing pages, poorly formatted text, programming characters, etc…. will all hurt your search engine ranking. By submitting an incomplete website you risk getting penalized by the search engines. Consider how irritating it is when you are looking for information and you come across several web sites that are incomplete and useless.

- **Longevity** –Longevity does count and the longer your website has been online the higher it will be ranked in most major search engines. As stated above; unfinished pages will adversely affect ranking, so avoid posting pages that are under construction. However, publish the majority of your website and add pages as they are completed.

- **Add fresh content regularly** –the addition of new content signifies to search engines that the site is active and can give a tremendous boost in ranking. Search engine spiders index websites regularly if the content changes often the website will get indexed more frequently and receive a higher ranking. This is why having dynamic content is so important.

- **Increase your link popularity** –Link popularity is the measure of the number of external Websites that link to your site. This does not include links from within your own website. Do not confuse this with how many sites your website links to. From the search engines perspective, if there are many websites that link to your website, your website must be important. If you link to other websites it benefits of them and not you.

- **Blog** –Blogs are terrific for increasing site ranking. Content can be easily updated regularly (provided you actually post). This ensures that your website will be indexed frequently. Blogs usually contain a lot of text so they are easily indexed by search engines.

163

- **Join community forums** –while not quite as effective as blogs, community forums are a powerful tool that can drastically improve your page ranking. Avoid blatant advertising in favor of having conversations online with other members about whatever topic is being discussed. Traffic can be gained by adding a simple hyperlink to your signature. Not only will you get a modest amount of direct traffic you will help improve your link popularity.

- **Meta tags, domain names and titles** – search engines also take in to account you domain name, the title of your page, and many other factors that may not be apparent to the casual user. If your keywords exist in the page title it signifies to the search engine the purpose of the page and therefore gives special consideration to those keywords. This is also true for your domain name. If text is differentiated by heading tags or other formatting elements then those words are also considered more important by the search engines.

- **Don't bet on it** –what is true today may not hold water tomorrow. Most search engines change the algorithms used to determine ranking regularly. Generally, the exact algorithms and parameters used to determine rankings are not published. Therefore results change often and a website that is ranked number one on Tuesday may be ranked 10,000 on Wednesday. This is known as the search engine shuffle and in the case of Google, the Google Dance. So there is no guarantee and information may or may not be valid.

There are new and interesting strategies being developed all the time, so it is a good idea to stay informed about new developments and techniques, so remember to bookmark my website www.EverMoreTech .com/SEO.

It is one thing to design develop and publish an outstanding site, it's another to drive traffic to it. Regardless of the quality of your website, if nobody sees it, it is useless. So even if your website is the most awesome website ever created, it will not do anybody any good if and nobody can find it.

Several of these topics and more will be covered in more depth in the following chapters.

CHAPTER THIRTY

TRADITIONAL MARKETING

Traditional marketing does not have the same kind of impact online as it does in the real world. Generally, it is harder to achieve results for a web site than it is for brick and mortar type business. This is largely due to the fact that it is difficult to get a person to visit your website using traditional advertising.

However, traditional marketing can play a vital and imperative role in advertising your website. As more people are becoming web savvy they are more inclined to go online for their needs. As a result traditional marketing techniques are becoming more productive. However, at this time, unless you have a very large marketing budget you should be frugal regarding traditional marketing techniques.

Regardless of your focus, you should include your website address, e-mail address and any other pertinent information in all of your traditional marketing particularly:

- Business cards
- Flyers
- Yellow page ads
- Radio, and television ads
- Vinyl Banners
- Telemarketing

- Faxes, mailers
- Vinyl automotive lettering

After all, any publicity is good publicity. It is just a matter of tracking your results so you can spend your marketing dollars most effectively.

It is important to include your online identity in all your marketing efforts. If you are already having something printed or advertised there is usually no extra cost involved to add your website and/or e-mail address.

There are many reasons for this: owning a website enhances your professional image. Besides, you never know, they might just visit. Additionally, if they use your services and file your business card away then they will always be able to reference your site if they are actively looking for you. Moreover, if they scan your business card there's a good chance your website address will automatically turn into a link when the card is processed….

Again whatever the reason, even if it's just one visitor, you should make it easy as possible to find and use your website.

CHAPTER THIRTY-ONE

GUERRILLA MARKETING

So if traditional marketing isn't going to help you what then, should you do? Guerrilla and other online marketing techniques can be cost effective and extremely successful. Often, they simply just make good sense. Your potential customer/client is already sitting at the computer and all it takes is a quick impulse to click a link leading to your website.

There are many techniques that you can use to market your site online. Some are more effective than others. It will be up to you to determine what works best for you and your site. Fortunately to help you determine this there are many tools available online. Visit www.EverMoreTech.com/Marketing to see a current list of some of these techniques and the tools that you can use to track them.

Basically marketing your website online takes time, effort, patience, tenacity, and money. To simplify this, it can be boiled down to time vs. money. When considering online marketing time and money are proportional. If you can invest more money it will require less time. The opposite holds true if you can invest more time an effort into your marketing campaign it will require less money.

If you have money to work with, there are many tools and programs that you can work with. Pay per click advertising, banners, production companies, professional SEO companies are among some of the choices that will be available to you. With a decent marketing budget successfully driving traffic to your website can be much easier. However you will still need to spend your money wisely.

On the other hand, if you have a limited budget there are still many things that you can do. Many of these things will produce outstanding results, but they will require some effort on your part. Most of these options are based around social networking and blogging. Your results will depend on how much effort in time you are able to devote to your marketing campaign.

Let's take a look at some of your options so you can better determine how to use your resources.

Low cost/no cost solutions most of these solutions can be very effective without breaking the bank.

- **Search engine optimization (manually)** by researching various techniques and using some freely available tools to help you, you can work and optimizing your site for several key words. With patience and tenacity you should see some results.

- **Reciprocal linking** many webmasters in similar but not competing businesses to yours may be interested in the link exchange. Simply contact the webmaster (there's usually a link to do just that at the bottom of most web sites) and ask if he is interested in the link exchange.

- **Newsletters** most web hosting companies provide the ability to compile a mailing list included with their regular hosting package. If you spend some time and develop a useful newsletter that you can send out periodically, you can offer to user articles that link back to your website that can attract new visitors.

- **Blogging** this is one of my favorites. It is easy and free to set up a blog (I have a great tutorial on this at www.EverMoreTech.com/tutorials that can help you get started). By spending a few moments every day or two Blogging, you can generate a good deal of traffic without spending a penny.

- **Community forums** are very similar to blogs, but they are more focused on a community discussion than a blog.

- **Press Releases** there are a multitude of newspapers, publications and web sites that are starving for content. If you publish some press releases and make them available to these publications you might benefit from some free advertising while they get some free content.

- **Word of mouth & Viral Campaigns** if you are fortunate enough to have one of your advertising campaigns go viral your traffic to go through the roof. Word of mouth is a very powerful factor in marketing. If the word gets around a community that your website is "cool" or has some kind of hook you may just find that community talking, chatting and blogging about your site. This is known as viral marketing and can reach millions of people.

- **Google AdWords** this program by Google can be extremely effective and do the fact that you can control how much you spend makes it available to many people. If you have a modest budget you can usually find a few keywords to bid on that will perform effectively for you. However, if your try to compete for highly popular keywords this may be too expensive. So if you find that your keywords are not performing or you're not getting enough bang for your buck, revise your keywords.

- **Sponsorships** there is no shortage of community minded organizations and another good causes online and in the real world that value sponsorships. By donating goods, time, or professional services and or money, many nonprofit or other sites for worthy causes will place a banner and or links to your company on their Website. Not only does this tend to be cost effective parentheses or perhaps not, but that depends on how philanthropic you are) and you get the extra added benefit of having your ad placed on a Website for a worthy cause. Needless to say; this engenders trust in the community and typically have sow people that need it. Sites looking for sponsors can range from your local little league, helping the homeless, battered women's shelters etc....

Large budget solutions

- **Banner advertising** I include this in the large budget category because it typically takes a large number of banners across multiple sites to see a substantial result from banner advertising. This is not always the case however and sometimes banner advertising works on a smaller budget...

- **Google AdWords** I have included AdWords in both categories because it is it effective with virtually any budget. However if the sky's the limit, you can be certain of generating traffic.

- **Paid links** the problem with reciprocal linking is twofold: first you have to provide the website that you are linking with a link back. This may not be advisable or even possible. Secondly, most of the time the link pointing to you is placed on an insignificant link page that is buried somewhere within the site. However if you have the budget you can simply offer to pay to have your links included on other websites. You can even go one step further and pay to have them add some content that features your website.

- **Flash banner advertising** I differentiate flash banner advertising from regular banner advertising due to the fact that flash banners offer the ability to program small web applications right into the banner. This allows the banner to do things such as expand or allow people to play a game. By making the banner interactive flash banners tend to be more successful.

- **Professional Newsletter Service** there are many companies that offer professional newsletter services. Most of them will offer a template that can be easily customized and sent out to thousands if not millions of people. Be careful to make certain to send your information in the form of a newsletter rather than an advertisement. As you can probably guess people dislike getting spam. However, if you are sending a useful and informative newsletter people actually look forward to receiving it

- **Professional Blogging Service** it is possible to hire an individual or service to blog for you. Prices and qualities vary greatly in range so be careful. Make sure that you can approve whatever material is created for your blog before it is posted. It can be unprofessional to have incorrect information published on your blog in your name.

- **Video advertising** in addition to television the Internet has become a viable medium for video advertising.   Youtube.com and other video oriented websites make it possible to inexpensively promote your business and/or website through the use of video.

These are just a few ideas to help get you started. Again, the only limitation is that of your imagination. Think of new ways to use existing technologies and solutions by combining them are doing something slightly different or look for totally new and revolutionary methods of promoting your website. The Internet is growing so rapidly that innovation is never far away.

Focusing your marketing efforts online can be very productive. After all, it is very difficult to motivate a person to visit your website after seeing it in print or hearing it on the radio. It is much easier to take advantage of the impulse to simply click a link. For instance, how many times has somebody handed you a business card with a website address on it and has encouraged you to visit their website... How many times have you actually done so? Most people would say "rarely". How about you, yourself, how many links have you clicked this past week?

If money is no object (I wish I had this problem) then there are a number of things that you can do. There are Millions of Website owners that would be happy to run a banner advertising campaign for a fee. There are a few common pricing models for banner campaigns:

- **Pay per impression** under this sort of a plan you are charged based on how many times your ad is displayed. In other words; if the website you are advertising on displays your banner 100,000 times and charges you $25.00 per thousand it would cost you $4,000.00 to run the ad. There is little or no guarantee of success. Regardless of the number of impressions, you have to pay the same amount of money whether or not anybody actually clicks on your ads.

- **Pay per click** as the name suggests pay per click programs charge the advertiser every time a user clicks on the ad. This is usually a good choice because you are paying for direct results.

- **Flat rate** no surprises here. Flat rate pricing is just that. A set price per month, week, or year regardless of how many impressions and/or clicks.

Of course there are many other ways of marketing your website. If you are creative, and you don't mind spending a little bit of time the results can pay off handsomely.

One thing to consider; although most people think of e-mail when they hear the word spam, it also applies to many other tactics sometimes employed in online marketing. For instance, the practice of falsely optimizing your site for search engines is known as search engine spanning. Also, posting advertisements to a Committee for OM not related to the discussion is known as board spamming the stand a good chance of being banned from that form.

Additionally there are other techniques that people use to promote their product are website that are simply annoying, ineffective, or just plain unscrupulous. Do yourself a favor and practice good netiquette. If you're not sure whether not you should run a particular ad campaign, use this rule of thumb; if it bugs you, it will probably bug your potential visitors.

Be smart when using creative marketing techniques online. If you're going to use a community forum; join the discussion and say nothing about your business, but be sure to include a link to your website in your signature. Community forums are there for a purpose and that purpose is not to advertise your business. However, if your post is part of the discussion, nobody (typically) will have a problem with your link. If your link remains an all odds are good that Google will index your link and improve your link popularity.

It is important to keep in mind that you are not after direct traffic. You should be attempting to improve your placement within the search engines. So our goal here is to improve link popularity and that is done by getting your links on is many websites as possible. Remember, the higher the site is ranked, the more valuable a link from that site is.

Likewise, the same principle applies to blogging. If you are posting articles to your blog that are simply advertisements for your website, your blog will probably not be very compelling. If your blog is not interesting it won't be very useful to you either. This is because it will probably have a low page rank and therefore not very much impact on your link popularity. Not only that, but it is not likely to generate much interest in the way of direct traffic to your website.

GOOGLE ADWORDS

The Google AdWords™ program is a very effective pay per click advertising program. Google™ provides advertising using the concept called contextual advertising. In simpler terms this refers to a method of delivering ads based on the content of a website or search term.

For example; if a user visits Google™ and searches for lawn mowers; advertisements about lawnmowers and similar things up here in various places within the search results page. In short, advertisements are based on the context of the page. This is an extremely effective technique as it delivers ads pertaining to exactly what the reader is looking for. This ensures that advertisements are shown to people that are probably interested in them.

Furthermore, Google™ has taken great pains to make sure that it is only serving suitable, quality ads. Every ad is scrutinized to ensure that is not breaking Google's Terms of Service. This helps ensure there is no pornography, ad spam, viruses or obvious scams. Additionally, Google not only filters the ads it serves, it won't allow its advertising to run on sites that contain pornography or unsuitable content.

For these reasons, people generally trust ads by Google and are comfortable clicking them. In contrast, in the early days of banner advertising, it was all too common to click an ad only to have hundreds of other ads popup uncontrollably.

This nearly killed linked and banner advertising altogether and certainly gave even the most honest online advertisers a real black eye. It became very difficult to run an online advertising campaign for legitimate companies as the public became leery of all online advertising.

Ultimately this adversely affected the number of people that were clicking on ads, so rendered it completely ineffective and a virtual waste of money to run a banner ad campaign in the late nineties.

The Google AdSense™ program was very well received. In the beginning it only used subtle text ads. This coupled with the fact that most people knew Google's reputation and they began clicking again.

It was soon obvious that online advertisers had a new and effective way to reach customers. Once again, the online advertising model was profitable. Effectively this gave the Internet's and the tech industry in general a much needed shot in the arm after the.com bubble burst. Clearly it made sense to advertise online again.

All you need to get started with your own account is to visit http://Google.com/adwords. It is free to sign up and you can start receiving traffic today. Take your time and develop a good list of keywords. Be sure to include as many as you possibly can. There is a tutorial a tutorial at www.EverMoreTech.com/Tutorials that can help guide you through the whole process.

THE POWER OF BLOGGING

By now and I'm sure you've heard of blogging. In a nutshell obliged is an online diary, or web log. A blog makes it possible for user to post and publish just about anything regarding any topic they can think of online without the need to know anything more than how to surf the web. There are plenty of blog communities available that are free and easy to setup and use. Try Blogger.com or Wordpress.com for starters

People typically blog about things they know about and enjoy. Due to the fact that they already know what they're talking about it makes it easy to come up with new content.   Maintaining a blog that is updated frequently will generally lend a degree of respectability online. Readers usually begin to feel comfortable and familiar with the blogger. Furthermore, each blog entry (assuming you include a link or two to your website) essentially adds to link popularity and thereby increases page ranking. Additionally, you are likely to receive some direct traffic as well.

If used right blogging can be a powerful tool in your overall marketing strategy.

As mentioned earlier, you can start your own blog for free. There are many services online that provide free blogs that you can customize as you see fit. It only takes about ten minutes to set up a new blog. All you need to do is simply   sign up with the blogging service of your choice. Then you   can start posting.

With the Google AdSense™ program you can run ads by Google on your blog and/or website. If you do, every time a visitor clicks on an ad Google will pay you a percentage of the revenue that the click generated.

In simpler terms, if you run ads for Google™ then Google is willing to share a piece of the pie. It is also free to join and easy to sign up. Once you have in AdSense account most blogs have a simple tool to put AdSense on your pages.

Finally, Blogging is kind of fun. If you like writing at all blogging can be quite enjoyable. Try it and see for yourself...

CHAPTER THIRTY-TWO

ONLINE COMMUNITIES

*A*lso known as forums, online communities when used properly are a powerful tool that can help you in many ways. Ideally, you should belong to several online communities. There are online communities and forums covering just about every topic of imaginable.

Some online communities are thriving and are made up of several hundred or even thousands of members. These people are all sharing knowledge, experience and information regarding a common topic. In the past they were called bulletin boards or BBS systems. These terms are familiar if you've been around a really long time like I have.

There are many ways that community forums can help. Two ways are: one, when you have a question regarding your website, whether it's hosting, design, development, implementation etc.... then you can post a question and people from the community will usually answer it relatively quickly. A discussion board that has good participation will usually have your question answered within a couple hours, perhaps even minutes. Secondly, you can use discussion boards to promote your website. Beware of promoting your site too aggressively on discussion forums. If you do, you will probably be perceived as somebody that doesn't care about the community, but rather, is just out to advertise. This is considered "board spamming" and you are likely to get banned.

To elaborate on both these topics I should mention a few things. First, most online communities will have several members that are committed to maintaining the board. They are known as moderators and usually have the power to delete posts. So if you're looking for help, you will have better results if you introduce yourself and post a couple of topics.

It is called netiquette; in a nutshell it is just the practice being polite on the web. Think of it this way; if you met a doctor at a party, would you ask is professional advice about a personal condition? Most people would consider this pretty rude. Isn't it much more polite to strike up a conversation and get to know the person a little bit before you simply pick their brains for information? Of course, you should probably if call his office and make an appointment, but that is beside the point

The same principle applies online. As a professional, I answer a lot of people's questions and offer my assistance where I can. I personally do it because I like to give back to the community and it always feels good to help people out. However, when someone comes across as if they believe they are entitled to my time and knowledge it can be pretty irritating. Occasionally, some people can become downright rude. The old axiom *you catch more flies with honey than vinegar* certainly holds true online.

Keep this in mind when you are marketing on community forums. In general, the people that run online communities hate people that use their website to do nothing more than advertise. If you post a topic that is a shameless advertisement for your business or website you are likely to get flamed by other members and stand a good chance of getting banned by the moderators.

In fact, there are actually programs, known as bots, that do nothing other than sign up for online community accounts and post messages that make little or no sense but contain several links to various websites. If that was not bad enough, more often than not the links will go to Websites that are pornographic in nature. These posts have to be vigilantly guarded against and removed.

If you want to gain the fury and ire of an online community just post a message like; "visit my website for the best widgets on the planet at www.BuyMyWidgetsHere.com." If it is an active board your message will last about ten minutes before somebody comes and deletes it in bans you from ever posted on that board again.

Additionally, you risk alienating your potential clients...

The secret to using online communities to market your website is very simple. Most discussion boards have a control panel that will allow you to add a signature. This signature appears at the bottom of all of your posts. Simply make sure that your signature contains a link to your website.

Here's an example of a good signature that will both bring direct traffic to your site and increase your link popularity in the search engines;

> *Best regards,*
>
> *Marc Everlove*
> *Www.EverMoreTech.com Exploring Technology*
>
> *"IF YOU THINK YOU CAN OR YOU THINK YOU CAN'T, YOU'RE RIGHT." –HENRY FORD*

All you need to do is; participate in conversations about whatever interests you. It doesn't matter whether the topic is business, baseball or bungee jumping; you will be marketing your website and increasing your link popularity at the same time. Even better, you may learn a few things and even make a few new friends.

Online communities are fantastic tool that can help you in many different ways. I strongly encourage you to join several. You can start by joining mine at www.EverMoreTech.com Just register and you can begin posting. I'll see you online.

Chapter Thirty-Three

Freebies & Other Online Goodies

Over time , as your skills progress you will need and desire more comprehensive tools to do more with your website beyond the simple basics. Fortunately, there is a multitude of free tools and applications that will help you along your way. However, you have to be very careful regarding what you download, as some applications will contain viruses and spyware. Of course of on my Website EverMoreTech.com there is a list of a few freeware applications that I personally use and recommend. Amongst these are antivirus programs, HTML editors, browser plug-ins and assorted other useful items that are there completely free or low cost.

Additionally, there are countless other tools online that you may find on your own. Download at your own risk! Also, be wary of downloading pirated software or illegal software, not only is it illegal, but pirated software is a high risk to contain spyware and viruses.

Even though the threat of scams exists, there are several websites, newsletters and other services that will help you find great software at little or no cost. Often, you'll be able to find open source alternatives to commonly used expensive commercial software.

In fact in many cases the open source software actually rivals its commercial counterpart. While products like

Microsoft Office™ enjoy a position of dominance they can be pricey. Given its dominance as the de facto leader in word processors, it is hard to accomplish much without having Microsoft Office installed. However, with the emergence of open source software packages such as Open Office™ that can read and write Office™ files that are now cost effective alternatives.

Don't get me wrong, I like Microsoft™ products very much. Whenever possible I use them. With that said, I have worked with many clients that have had budget issues where such products made a lot of sense for them.

This is just one of many open source alternatives to commercial software available. There are many different operating systems, productivity suites, graphics programs and many other applications. If you play your cards right, you can save a great deal of money.

One word of warning though; some of these applications require a small amount of technical savvy. They are not commercial programs and rarely do they have official tech support. They do however; usually have online communities that will answer any questions that you may have. If you are not technically savvy, nor do you have someone who is at your disposal, you may want to use commercially available software where ever possible.

Using open source software is a good way to learn a lot about technology quickly. Even though it can be more difficult to install and maintain the online communities are generally very active and helpful. By dealing with the various issues that may arise with the help of the online community, you can learn all sorts of things.

There are many places to learn more about open source and other alternative programs. You can check out my website for starters. There are links to some of the programs and applications that I've used with great results.

CHAPTER THIRTY-FOUR

BLACK HATS, WHITE HATS & WHAT YOU SHOULD KNOW ABOUT THEM

When I mention the word hackers in front of a room of people, I usually get their attention quickly. The fact of the matter is while most people have a stereotypical view of hackers and believe all hackers are shadowy sinister types, bent on ruining people's lives. While this may be true in some cases, there is another side of the coin.

There are two major types of hackers. There are good guys, known as "white hats" and the bad guys, known as "black hats. The lines can get blurry sometimes, as some individuals will play both sides of the fence. Although hacking has a bad reputation; white hat hackers are the unsung heroes that help keep you safe online.

If we take a closer look we will find that there are different types of hacking. There is hardware modification, ethical hacking, security probing, penetration testing, Google hacking, etc.... Within the technical community hacking has a larger meaning than what is commonly accepted by the term itself. Essentially, hacking is the act of modifying something that already exists to make its suit your needs.

Hardware hacking front/modifications can be anything from extending the range of a garage door opener to

189

converting a moped to run on milk and anything in between. Ethical hacking is when a security firm or individual looks for exploits in applications and networks to expose them so that they may be repaired. Penetration testing is a type of ethical hacking that is usually done in the final stage of launching a web server, network, application or website to find any security vulnerabilities that might exist. Google hacking is the practice of using Google and other search engines to uncover systems that can be exploited, or find information the generally wasn't meant to be seen on the Internet.

In summary, White Hat Hackers are the folks that develop software that will protect you from their counterparts the Black Hat Hackers. Of course this leads to a sort of arms race like escalation with the Black Hats finding new exploits and developing new techniques versus the White Hats that are trying to detect intrusions and vulnerabilities, patch exploits and develop the other preventative measures to keep the Black Hats out. It is a classic castle vs. siege engine scenario with each side trying to outdo the other.

This should be of interest to you due to the fact that some of the easier and more popular hacks come from exploits of Websites. There are a few reasons for this: websites are accessible online, are written by people with varying degrees of programming ability, often access the database, and many times are not secured properly.

If a website is not written properly it is possibly open to several different kinds of attacks. Websites that use databases can be particularly vulnerable to attacks such as SQL injection, cross site scripting and others.

The little known fact is; the hacking community, both good and bad, is pretty well organized. There are Websites, tools, and even conventions on both sides.

As a small Website owner, you should be aware of some of the threats that exist. Most of the necessary security should be in place by your webmaster and your web host. If they do their jobs properly the most serious threats should be reasonably well secured. Even so, there is no network that is completely invulnerable.

If you are the owner of a large website, or you are enduring the painful experience of running your own web server then there are some serious concerns that you will need to address. However, that is outside the scope of this book. I recommend that you consult a professional security company to check out your website and make sure that is reasonably secure.

CHAPTER THIRTY-FIVE

SPAM, SCAMS & HOW TO PROTECT YOURSELF

One of the more serious issues that can be quite a nuisance is the influx of unwanted e-mail that may fill your inbox once you have an e-mail address published online. This can be a real problem may cause a number of issues.

It is very difficult to stop once it starts. When your e-mail address gets compromised and added to mailing lists your options are somewhat limited. The best defense is to make sure that you don't get on a mailing list. There are few tools and safe practices that you can use to help minimize your exposure.

Mailing lists will gather e-mail addresses from a number of sources. Once you have a registered domain name you can bet your website will be visited by a "bot" that harvests e-mail addresses. These bots read the code that powers your website and strip all of the e-mail addresses out of it. These e-mail addresses can then be added to a database which is then used to send unsolicited e-mail. Before you know it your e-mail addresses have been sold and resold many times. The result is an enormous amount of spam that can overrun your inbox rendering it useless.

Your e-mail address can also be used to send a legitimate email to other people in some cases. If your mail server is not properly secured, your e-mail account could be used as a spam zombie. This is probably not the publicity you're looking for.

The best way to guard against this is to encode your e-mail within your websites code. There are a number ways and to do it and should be relatively easy for your webmaster to do it. One of the most common methods is to use a scripting language to create the e-mail address by adding two strings of text together. This will effectively safeguard your e-mail in most cases.

Many of you might be asking; "what about the unsubscribe button?" Many newsletters and e-mail lists may have a legitimate unsubscribe button where they actually works. However, unscrupulous list owners will simply use this as a way of verifying that is alive e-mail address and either disregard the unsubscribe request or simply sell the e-mail address to another mailing list company.

In essence the bad guys can use the unsubscribed link as a litmus test to validate their e-mail addresses. Ultimately, it is up to you whether not to use the unsubscribe link. In most cases it's OK, however the possibility does exist that it can cause even more spam.

HELPFUL TECHNIQUES

- **Concatenation of your e-mail address will help**. For those of you that speak actual in English this means to break up your e-mail address into separate parts and put it together via programming when it is needed. Your webmaster should be able to help you with this.
- **Use the e-mail aliases.** Using this technique will allow you to have multiple accounts forward to one account. The benefit; important business contacts, family, friends can have your main e-mail address, while your other e-mail addresses can be abandoned or changed if necessary. By using this technique you will not need to update your contact information anywhere except on your website. The abandoned e-mail addresses can remain active with stronger spam filters on them for as long as you deem appropriate to make sure you don't lose any important messages.
- **Use Forms and redirects**. By using a form or some other type of script that sends the users request for e-mail communication with you to an entirely separate page effectively hides your e-mail address from the majority of e-mail harvesting programs.
- **Use an online mail client to filter your messages.** By using a major Internet mail client to retrieve your mail you can take advantage of their powerful spam filters. I personally use Gmail and have been very impressed by the accuracy of their spam filters.

In summary, spam is a problem that is best dealt with before it's a problem. Once it gets out of hand there's very little you can do about it. Hopefully, as time progresses, spam filters become more powerful and people become savvier spam will not be such a problem. However, you should take the steps necessary to minimize your exposure.

CHAPTER THIRTY-SIX

GENERATION X & Y: THE WEB SAVVY CUSTOMER

speak to many people every day that would like Websites but they are nervous because they don't know much about technology or they believe they can get along with business as usual. While this may be true for some people, more people are using the Internet regularly to find and buy goods and services that they use to find conventionally. It is quite evident that this trend will continue, therefore it is safe to say that if you plan to do business in the future, most likely, you will need a Website. And since that is the case the sooner you start the more of an advantage you will have over your competition.

The X and Y generations tend to do business differently than previous generations. The younger generations have grown up being exposed to technology early on. They generally are more comfortable using it and have less difficulty understanding it. Future generations are likely to be even more technically oriented. Considering the spending power of the stenographic it is wise to be as prepared as possible.

It doesn't matter what your occupation is. If you sell or manufacture a product you should probably have a website that can handle ecommerce. If you are a service provider you will want to make sure people can find you online.

Conventional methods of doing business are under siege. Increasing numbers of consumers look for business phone numbers and addresses online. Many people are using mobile devices and can access the Internet from anywhere. It is easier for the average tech-savvy person to find something using their mobile phone then it is for them to find and search through the conventional phone book for a business. Additionally, they can find out more about a business online then they can in the phonebook.

Web savvy clients will probably want to know what services you offer and what they can expect to pay for your services and other details about your business. This can be a huge advantage over your competition that has not posted a website yet. They simply cannot make that kind of information available without a site, nor can they compete with a global reach of the Internet.

Consider this; a web savvy individual can use is smart phone or mobile device to order pizza, checks his online bill pay service and select a few DVDs from Netflix™ while he is standing in line at the grocery store. By the time he gets home the pizza has arrived and is and paid for, a couple of DVDs have been delivered to the mail and he doesn't have to pay the bills tonight.

The methods and accessibility of doing business online is bound to increase and becomes simpler and more efficient. The younger generations have proven their willingness to do business online.

If you sell something or if your service is available online, your market becomes global the moment you go online website online. The potential is as large and exciting as it seems. The only boundaries are only limited by your imagination.

This does not mean that if you want to website you will automatically be successful. However, in order to competitively do business in the new marketplace a website will be essential. The absence of a website in this new and evolving economy could spell disaster.

The fact of the matter is; the Internet has forever changed the way we do business. As technology evolves businesses will need to adapt and take advantage of these changes in order to prosper and grow. Fortunately owning and operating a website today is relatively inexpensive and there are many tools at your disposal.

The advantages of having an online presence in most cases far outweigh the challenges and cost of running Website. Maintaining an online presence gives you a tremendous advantage over your competition that does not. Every day that goes by solidifies your position in the search engines and puts you that much farther ahead.

200

CHAPTER THIRTY-SEVEN

PDAS, NOTEBOOKS, CELLS & MOBILITY

*Y*ou can see them cropping up everywhere... At your local coffee shop, café, mall etc... Just about everywhere, people are quietly setting off to the side hammering away on their mobile devices, laptops and net books.

Internet enabled cell phones and other wireless devices are rapidly gaining popularity as more and more devices become Internet capable and even more importantly, chic. Text messages, mobile websites and portable computing have found its way into the mainstream.

It's easy to see why. My cell phone is equipped with GPS and so I can get directions to get wherever I want to go from wherever I am (considering my crummy navigational skills this is a real boon for me, just ask my wife). The other day I was at a local sporting goods store buying baseball's for the little league team that I coach. They seemed a bit expensive so I did a quick price check from another sporting goods store across town. As a result I was able to get the baseballs and treat the team to a pizza party after the game.

It seems that there is no end to what can be accomplished with mobile computing. I can add content to my website from the road. Text messaging can be incredibly useful. Not to mention the ability to retrieve

201

e-mail from practically anywhere. The possibilities for and potential uses of technology is seemingly limitless.

Keeping this in mind that is important to include a set of pages designed for mobile devices when you are creating your website. Currently, in some situations, the limitations of mobile devices make it necessary to have a special section or parallel website that is specifically targeted for more mobile devices. If this is the case, you ensure that your mobile users will have a good experience with their website.

The secret is using minimal graphics optimized for small screens which are usually about 320 pixels wide. If you can keep your content in this kind of a framework it will enable mobile web pages to load faster. This will provide a much better experience for users with mobile devices.

Chapter Thirty-Eight

Webmaster Tools & Other Useful Things

*A*t this point you may have already completed your website, or you may be nearing completion. While we have covered a lot of information regarding how important rankings are, it is time to take a look at some tools that will be useful for increasing your website's ranking.

There are literally millions of free tools available online that you can use to enhance your website. HTML editors, traffic analyzers, code snippets, web applications, color pickers, RS as feeds and a host of others. Visit my website EverMoreTech.Com for list of useful tools that you can download for free.

A couple tools that I should mention here are Google's Webmaster Tools™ and Analytics™. Google's Webmaster Tools™ contains a set of tools that can help you maintain and run your website effectively. This set contains tools to help you create and submit a site map for Google™ which will help you with your site ranking. When coupled with the Google Analytics™ which contains outstanding set of tools that will come in handy analyzing and optimizing traffic. Available for free online, Google Analytics™ and Webmaster Tools™ are a "must have" if you are serious about your website.

CHAPTER THIRTY-NINE

REDESIGNS, UPGRADES & KEEPING FRESH

Once you have created and launch your website, you should always strive to keep your content fresh and up to date. Upon completion of your Website, and after you have: optimized it for search engines, marketed it, labored over press releases, exchanged links, you may finally be getting some decent traffic, it is important to continue updating your content appropriately. Static websites will need less maintenance than dynamic websites, but in either case it is a good idea to keep with the times.

If you keep your site up-to-date you stand a good chance of receiving return traffic. However, if you allow your website to become outdated then it is unlikely that your visitors will return.

Even worse, if you're website does not contain new content periodically the search engines will index it less frequently. Additionally, you will not be getting the most possible from your website.

If you have a content management system or framework type website than you can change your content yourself. Otherwise you may have to payee someone to do it. In any case make sure that the information contained on your website is relevant in up to date.

If you have a community driven website than the content is not a problem. Fortunately for you the members of your website will be providing fresh content regularly. In the case of community driven sites, it is relatively difficult to get it can be a challenge to reach that point. To expect any sort of community participation there needs to be a considerable amount of content to begin with, otherwise, there is simply not much to talk about. So, even with a community driven website you can still look forward to providing content, at least in the beginning.

Now that you have your website, what you do with it is up to you. If you build a good website, market it well and keep it up to date, you can compete with giants.

I wish you the best of luck in your endeavors and I hope this information will prove to be useful to you. Also that your website will be a success!

I hope to see you online at www.EverMoreTech.com! Stop by the community forum and post a link to your website so that we can all see it.

Again, best of luck and happy surfing!

APPENDIX ONE:

IMPORTANT POINTS TO REMEMBER

- Develop an easy to remember Username/Password scheme. Remember to have a unique username and an eight or more character password with at least one capital letter and one number or symbol.

- Buy a bound notebook and record all relevant information regarding your website, webmaster, domain name and hosting account.

- Choose your webmaster wisely. Make sure you can understand him and that he answers your questions effectively.

- Take time to plan. If you have a good image of what you want your website to look like and what you want it to accomplish then you are setting yourself up for success.

- Create accounts at some different stock graphic websites and browse the images that are available. You can bookmark the ones you like and share the information with your webmaster. It is cheaper than having a photographer furnish the graphics and will give your webmaster valuable insight as to what you want your site to look like.

- Know your audience! Design your site accordingly. For instance, is your intended audience tech savvy, business oriented, artistic, young, old, etc... Take into consideration any special factors and design your website to benefit your expected visitors.

- Get a backup copy of your entire website. Make sure to update this often if your content changes a lot.

- Check out your website in different browsers and make sure that the design does not "break" or in the worst case it "fails gracefully."

- Develop a marketing plan based on the amount of time and money you can dedicate to your website. Remember, when the website is finished the work has really only begun.

- Use whatever free marketing opportunities that you can think of. Community forums, blogs, press releases and other guerilla marketing techniques can be very effective when used properly.

- Monitor your progress by using an application to read your web site statistics. There are many tools online that can help you track and analyze your website traffic. You can find more information about this on my website www.EverMoreTech.com

APPENDIX TWO:

COMMON HTML TAGS

<!-- *COMMENT GOES HERE* --> COMMENT –USED TO ADD A COMMENT TO THE CODE. ANYTHING BETWEEN THE STAGS WILL BE DISREGARDED BY THE BROWSER. NOTICE THAT THIS PARTICULAR TAG IS DIFFERENT. THE CONTENT GOES IN BETWEEN THE OPENING AND CLOSING BRACKET.

<!DOCTYPE> Document Type – this tag lets the browser know what kind of document it is.

<a></a> Anchor – specifies an anchor point.

<abbr> </abbr> Abbreviation – specifies an abbreviation.

Acronym – specifies an acronym.

<address> – specifies an address.

<applet> – specifies an applet. This tag has been depreciated in favor of the script tag.

<area>—used to define an area in an image map.

<b>—used to set the font weight to bold

<base>—specifies a address that is default for the page

<bdo>—if specifies text direction

<big>—sets font size too big

<blockquote>—specifies along quotation.

<body>—signifies the body area of a web page.

—creates a single line break.

<button>—creates a simple push button. Typically used in forms.

<caption>—defines a caption

<center>—centers text

<cite>—designates a citation

<code>—formats text as computer code. Don't confuse this with script tags. This is to define or display text with special formatting to designate that it is computer code.

<col> defines attributes for column

<colgroup>—defines a group of columns.

<dd>—signifies a definition.

<del>—signifies deleted text

<dfn>—signifies a definition term

<dir>—creates a directory list

<div>—creates a division or section within the document

<dl>—creates a definition list

<dt>—the definition of a term within a definition list.

<em>—formats enclosed text with emphasis.

<fieldset>—adds a border to elements within a form.

<font>—allows a attributes to format text

<form>—defines a form within a document

<frame>—defines a frame within a frame set

<frameset>—allows multiple web pages to be displayed on one page in separate frames

<head>—defines the head section of an HTML document. This section allows the addition of scripts and other elements that do not belong within the body

210

\<h1\>—formats text as heading. Has levels one through six.

\<hr\>—creates a simple line across the page.

\<html\>—defines a document or portion of a document as HTML

\<i\>—formats enclosed text in Italics

\<iframe\>—defines and inline frame

\<img\>—specifies an image

\<input\>— defines an input control

\<ins\>—defines inserted text

\<label\>—specifies the label for a form element

\<legend\>—defines a caption within a fieldset

\<li\>—denotes a line item within a list

\<link\>—specifies relationship between an external or file and itself

\<map\>—denotes an image map.

\<menu\>—the notes a menu list of links.

\<meta\>—allows the addition of Meta data about the document

\<noframes\> specifies different content for browsers that do not support frames.

\<noscript\>—specifies different content for browsers that do not support scripts.

\<object\>—denotes and embedded object.

\<ol\>—creates a numbered list

\<optgroup\> defines a group of options in a select list

\<option\>—defines in option in a select list

<p>—creates a paragraph formatting elements

<param>—defines a parameter of an object

<s>—formats text and strikethrough

<script>—allows the addition of a client-side script

<select>—adds a drop down list

<small>—formats text as small

<span>—Spans another element or formatting

<strike>—formats text as strikethrough

<strong>—formats the text as strong

<style>—defines CSS information

<sub>—formats text in a subscript

<sup>—formats the text a superscript

<table>—defines a table

<tbody>—defines the body of a table

<td>—defines a table cell

<textarea>—creates a text area within a form

<title> defines the title of a nation EL document

<tr>—creates a row of cells within a table

<u>—formats text as underlined

<ul>—creates an unordered (bullet) list

APPENDIX 3:

HTML CODE FOR A BASIC WEBSITE TEMPLATE

This code is available for download at
WWW.evermoretech.com/codesamples

```
<!-- WHATEVER IT IS CONTAINED IN OR COMMENTS TO HELP YOU
UNDERSTAND WHAT THE REST OF THE CODE MEANS I WILL BREAK
IT ALL DOWN INTO SECTIONS AND EXPLAIN IT.  IF YOU HAVE
DOWNLOADED THE SOURCE CODE AND PASTE IT INTO NOTEPAD
DOCUMENT THE BROWSER WILL DISREGARD ANY COMMENTS IN
BETWEEN THESE TAGS -->

<!- THIS PORTION OF THE PAGE DEFINES THE TYPE OF
DOCUMENT.  IT IS NOT NECESSARY TO INCLUDE IT, BUT IT IS
GOOD FORM.-->

<!DOCTYPE html PUBLIC "-//W3C//DTD XHTML 1.0
Transitional//EN"
"http://www.w3.org/TR/xhtml1/DTD/xhtml1-
transitional.dtd">

<html xmlns="http://www.w3.org/1999/xhtml">

<!-- THIS IS THE HEAD SECTION.  IT CAN CONTAIN
INFORMATION ABOUT THE PAGE AND OTHER ELEMENTS THAT DO NOT
BELONG WITHIN THE BODY OF THE PAGE, SUCH AS; THE TITLE,
CSS, PROGRAMMING SCRIPT AND META INFORMATION. -->

<head>

<meta http-equiv="Content-Type"
content="text/html; charset=utf-8" />

<title>My First Webpage</title>

<style type="text/css">

<!--
```

```
.style1 {color: #FFFFFF}

-->

</style>

</head>
```

<!-- THIS IS THE BODY SECTION. IT CONTAINS THE BULK OF THE CODE. YOUR CONTENT AND STYLING INFORMATION GOES HERE. MOST TAGS CAN CONTAIN ONE OR MORE ATTRIBUTES THAT CAN MODIFY OR DEFINE ELEMENTS OF THAT TAG. FOR INSTANCE, IN THE BODY TAG BELOW THE FONT ATTRIBUTE HAS BEEN SET TO ARIAL AND THE FONT COLOR TO BLACK. UNLESS OTHERWISE SPECIFIED THIS WILL BE THE DEFAULT FOR THE DOCUMENT -->

```
<body font face="arial" color="black">
```

<!-- THIS IS A TABLE. IT WILL CONTAIN ONE OR MORE ROWS AND COLUMNS. THE RESULTING GRID MAKES INDIVIDUAL CELLS. AN INDIVIDUAL CELL CAN SPAN MULTIPLE COLUMNS OR ROWS. A CELL CAN CONTAIN VIRTUALLY ANY TYPE OF CONTENT INCLUDING ANOTHER TABLE. AS YOU SEE IN THE EXAMPLE BELOW A TABLE ROW TAG THAT FOLLOWED BY A CELL TAG DENOTES A CELL. A DIVISION IS CONTAINED WITHIN THE CELL AND IN IMAGE CONTAINED WITHIN THE DIVISION. -->

```
<table width="99%" border="0">

  <tr>

    <td colspan="2" bgcolor="#003399">

<div align="center">
```

<!- HERE IS AN IMAGE TAG. IT CONTAINS A PATH TO THE IMAGE AS WELL AS ANY ATTRIBUTES ABOUT THAT IMAGE. -->

```
<img
src="http://realestatetechonline.com/Framework/
0/Masthead875x130.jpg" alt="" name="Masthead"
width="875" height="130" id="Masthead"
style="background-color: #003399" />

</div><
```

```
/td>

  </tr>
```

```
<!--  THE CLOSING CELL AND TABLE ROW TAGS INDICATE THAT
DATA ROW IS CLOSED AND ALL ONLY CONTAINED ONE CELL.
THIS PARTICULAR CELL CONTAINS THE MASTHEAD THE NEXT
TABLE ROW TAG BEGINS A NEW ROW.  THE NUMBER OF COLUMNS
IN EACH ROW MUST BE EQUAL.  IT IS POSSIBLE TO SPAN A
COLUMN OR ROW, BUT ULTIMATELY IT MUST ALL ADD UP.-->
```

```
  <tr>

    <td><p> </p>
```

```
<!-THE TABLE BELOW IS LOCATED ON THE RIGHT HAND SIDE OF
THE PAGE IN THE FIRST CELL OF THE SECOND ROW.  THIS
TABLE CONTAINS MANY ROWS BUT ONLY ONE COLUMN.  EACH WILL
CONTAINS ONE LINK CREATING A BASIC NAVIGATION ELEMENT.--
>
```

```
      <table width="200" border="1"
cellpadding="7" cellspacing="7"
bordercolor="#FFFFFF">

        <tr>

          <td bordercolor="#000000"
bgcolor="#993300"><span class="style1"><a
href="http://evermoretech.com/book">Link
One</a></span></td>

        </tr>

        <tr>

          <td bordercolor="#000000"
bgcolor="#993300"><span class="style1"><a
href="http://evermoretech.com/book">Link
Two</a></span></td>

        </tr>

        <tr>
```

```
        <td bordercolor="#000000"
bgcolor="#993300"><span class="style1"><a
href="http://evermoretech.com/book">Link
Three</a></span></td>

        </tr>

        <tr>

        <td bordercolor="#000000"
bgcolor="#993300"><p class="style1"><a
href="http://evermoretech.com/book">Link
Four</a></p></td>

        </tr>

        <tr>

        <td bordercolor="#000000"
bgcolor="#993300"><span class="style1"><a
href="http://evermoretech.com/book">Link
Five</a></span></td>

        </tr>

        <tr>

        <td bordercolor="#000000"
bgcolor="#993300"><span class="style1"><a
href="http://evermoretech.com/book">Link
Six</a></span></td>

        </tr>

        <tr>

        <td bordercolor="#000000"
bgcolor="#993300"><span class="style1"><a
href="http://evermoretech.com/book">Link
Seven</a></span></td>

        </tr>

        <tr>

        <td bordercolor="#000000"
bgcolor="#993300"><span class="style1"><a
```

```
href="http://evermoretech.com/book">Link
Eight</a></span></td>

        </tr>

        <tr>

          <td bordercolor="#000000"
bgcolor="#993300"><span class="style1"><a
href="http://evermoretech.com/book">Link
Nine</a></span></td>

        </tr>

        <tr>

          <td bordercolor="#000000"
bgcolor="#993300"><span class="style1"><a
href="http://evermoretech.com/book">Link
Ten</a></span></td>

        </tr>

      </table>

    <p> </p></td>

<!--THE NAVIGATION ELEMENT ENDS WITH THAT FINAL CLOSING
CELL TAG.  THE REST OF THE CODE CONTAINS THE BULK OF THE
CONTENT. -->


    <td width="99%"><table width="99%"
border="0">

      <tr>

        <td><div id="lipsum">

          <p>Lorem ipsum dolor sit amet,
consectetur adipiscing elit. Quisque vitae arcu
vel purus fermentum vehicula. Phasellus ac
turpis id orci ultrices consequat.  Maecenas a
enim ut augue lobortis feugiat. Pellentesque
nec massa sed magna  ornare egestas. Fusce
enim. Praesent luctus. Vivamus id elit et
```

sapien elementum   ullamcorper. Aenean
consequat mauris sit amet ligula. Vestibulum
dignissim sem   ut metus. Fusce ligula nisi,
ullamcorper a, pretium nec, fringilla eu, nisl.
Nunc eleifend. Suspendisse placerat eros quis
mauris. Aliquam et purus at magna   ullamcorper
semper. Nulla facilisi. Praesent accumsan
vulputate ipsum. Cras sed   leo. Suspendisse
vel tortor a magna dictum euismod. Nullam at
justo eu dui   dignissim mollis. </p>

```
<table width="150" border="1"
align="left" cellpadding="3" cellspacing="3">

        <tr>

        <td><img
src="http://rockcat.als.lib.wi.us:90/screens/im
ages/pictureit.jpg" alt="Generic image"
width="150" height="150" /></td>

        </tr>

        </table>
```

<p>Suspendisse dui. Cras ullamcorper
scelerisque felis. Quisque in tortor.
Pellentesque varius fringilla enim. Suspendisse
potenti. Aliquam eleifend   rhoncus ante.
Vestibulum pharetra porttitor libero. Etiam
varius porttitor   metus. Etiam ut turpis.
Nullam facilisis, nisi nec tincidunt dictum,
nisi lacus   aliquam elit, ac fringilla velit
orci eget ligula. Etiam pulvinar pharetra nibh.
Donec porta. Nullam metus elit, euismod vel,
sollicitudin ut, auctor sed, urna.   Nullam
augue. Praesent quis mauris. Nunc ut sem vitae
nulla posuere semper.   Aliquam porta velit
quis purus. Nunc erat massa, posuere quis,
tempus rhoncus,   dictum at, velit. </p>

<p>Vivamus sed dui non orci rhoncus
elementum. Praesent fermentum. Donec libero.
In hac habitasse platea dictumst. Aenean
aliquet risus in nisi. Duis eget erat.
Quisque ultricies libero eu orci. Sed ultricies

tortor nec libero. Aliquam dignissim
tincidunt arcu. Praesent et nisi. In sed est
sed odio cursus lacinia. Donec porta justo
quis leo. Sed leo. Proin rhoncus ornare risus.
Mauris condimentum urna non tellus. In dictum
tellus eget nibh. Etiam tincidunt, diam ac
pulvinar egestas, lacus nulla ultrices enim,
quis tempor lectus lacus nec tortor. In
pretium, neque non egestas consectetur, massa
massa fermentum erat, at aliquet risus tellus
ac magna. Nam iaculis. Pellentesque adipiscing
venenatis orci. </p>

      <p>Praesent tristique. Curabitur
hendrerit tellus et lectus. Cras vel nisi nec
nibh viverra eleifend. Sed et velit eget lorem
cursus sollicitudin. Phasellus eleifend.
Quisque faucibus. Integer urna odio, tempor ac,
blandit quis, adipiscing eget, odio. Aliquam
odio metus, vulputate sit amet, eleifend ac,
mollis at, eros. Proin elementum metus sit amet
leo. Donec commodo aliquam arcu. Curabitur at
risus ac ipsum tempor lacinia. Proin aliquam
dolor eu erat. Class aptent taciti sociosqu
ad litora torquent per conubia nostra, per
inceptos himenaeos. Nullam eros ante, porta
sit amet, consequat et, ornare a, lacus.
Phasellus semper. Suspendisse laoreet, eros at
sollicitudin condimentum, sapien tortor
laoreet mauris, nec suscipit justo ligula sit
amet nibh. Maecenas velit lectus, condimentum
nec, interdum at, dictum in, velit. Aenean
massa purus, suscipit ac, ultrices quis,
bibendum et, lacus. </p>

      <p>Suspendisse potenti. Donec
interdum interdum augue. Quisque est. Nunc
rutrum neque id mi. Praesent ultricies
accumsan orci. Cras non diam. Nulla lobortis mi
non magna. Vestibulum volutpat gravida nibh.
Aenean mollis. Nulla nec mi. Nulla nunc. Sed
justo nibh, gravida id, tristique ut, tempor a,
urna. Cum sociis natoque penatibus et magnis
dis parturient montes, nascetur ridiculus mus.
</p>

```
            </div></td>
        </tr>
      </table></td>
    </tr>
    <tr>
      <td colspan="2"> </td>
    </tr>
  </table>
  </body>
  </html>
```

GLOSSARY

1337 – See *Leet.*

ADA Compliance – Requires websites to comply with the Americans with Disabilities Act of 1990.

AdWords™ – Google® advertising program that allows website owners to bid on specific keywords for placement of sponsored links.

Ajax –Programming language commonly used in website development and web apps.

Apache HTTP server – A popular general purpose web server.

API – Also known as an *Application Programming Interface*. An API enables interaction between separate applications.

ASP.net – A Web application framework published by Microsoft™. Aids developers in building web applications and dynamic websites.

Bandwidth – This is a measure of the amount of data you can send over a network.

Black Hats – Also known as Black Hat Hackers. Hackers that are attempting to gain access for illegal purposes.

Black Lists – A list of email servers that are known to be spam zombies. The mail server will not accept email from other mail servers on its blacklist.

Blog – A web log. Blogs can be published by anyone and contain information about anything.

Board Spamming – Posting links or advertising a business, product or website on a community forum.

Browser – Application used to view web pages and HTML files.

Cascading Style Sheets – Used to define and alter HTML tags and classes.

Cell – An individual section of an HTML table.

Client Side Script – A program or script that is executed on the user's machine rather than on the server. This requires the server to do less work and allows it to use its resources for other purposes.

CMS – See *Content Management System*

Co-location – The practice of leasing or selling a server located in a data center.

Content Management System – A website that allows a user or administrator to easily add, change, or delete content from a website.

Cross Browser Compatiblity – A term to describe a website that works in different browsers

CSS – See *Cascading Style Sheets*

Database – An application that provides a way of storing data

Database Driven Sites – A website that connects to a database to retrieve or store content

Dedicated Server – A server at provided by a web host that is solely dedicated to one website or client

DNS –See *Domain Name System*

Domain Name System – A system of Name Servers that resolve domain names into IP addresses

Domain Registrar – A provider of domain names

Dynamic Website – A website in which the content changes regularly

Email Alias – An email address that redirects messages to the actual email address.

Email Server – A server that can send and receive email.

File Extension – The last three or four characters after the dot in a filename that signify what application is used to open the file

File Transfer Protocol – Used to transfer files to and from web servers.

Flash™ – An application produced by Adobe® that can be used to create rich internet content

FTP – See *File Transfer Protocol*

HTML – See *Hypertext Markup Language*

Hypertext Markup Language – A standardized set of tags that modify simple text documents. HTML is the basic language of the World Wide Web.

IIS – See *Internet Information Server*

Interface – A tool that allows a user to use a program. It usually contains icons or other graphics that allow the user to access the different features of the application.

Internet Information Server – A popular web server produced by Microsoft®

 IP Address – An acronym for Internet Protocol Address. An address that a computer uses to send and receive data across a TCP/IP network such as the Internet

Java – A programming language often used on the World Wide Web.

JavaScript – A scripting language often used within web pages to allow a degree of functionality.

Key words – A set of words or phrases that define the main topic of a website. Often defined in the websites *Meta Tags.*

LEET – A common substitution cipher in which words are deliberately misspelled and letters are substituted by different characters that have a similar appearance to the letter it is replacing. Also known as 1337.

Linux – A computer operating system.

Link Popularity – A measure of how popular a website is based on how many other websites are linking to it.

Logic – The method used to solve an issue with programming code.

Mail Server – See *Email Server*

Meta Tag – An HTML tag in the head section of a website containing information regarding that website.

MySQL® – An open source database

MS SQL – A Microsoft® database

Netiquette – A term meaning *Internet Etiquette* –An unwritten set of rules governing expected behavior online.

Name Server – A server that resolves domain names into IP addresses. While any DNS server can be referred to as a name server, it is typically used in reference the DNS server that has authority over a domain. *i.e. You must point the Name Servers to your domain, so your visitors can access it online.*

Open Source – Software published with a license permitting the alteration of the source code. This type of software allows developers to make changes and alterations to the application. The software is typically distributed free of charge.

Organic Listings – Search engine rankings that occur naturally and are not paid for.

Parking Page – A page that is used as default for a website before the website is actually published.

Pay Per Click – A marketing campaign that allows a website owner to buy search engine placement. In this type of campaign, the website owner only pays for traffic he receives.

Pay Per Impression – A marketing campaign that allows a website owner to buy search engine placement. In this type of campaign, the website owner pays for traffic he receives.

Personal Web Server – A web server by Microsoft® that can be used with most Windows™ operating systems.

PHP – General purpose scripting language.

Python – A programming language

PWS – See *Personal Web Server*

Reciprocal Linking – The practice of trading links for better website search engine ranking.

Refresh Rate – The rate in which a monitor redraws the image on the screen.

Resolution – The number of pixels (or pixel dimension) a display.

Ruby – A programming language

Screen Resolution – is the number of dots that you see on your screen. The screen resolution determines how much "real estate" you have to work with. In other words on the same nineteen inch monitor you will have a larger area to work with at 1440 byte 1024 screen resolution than you would with an 800 by 600 screen resolution.

Script Light programming often included in websites.

Search Engine Optimization The practice of refining a website to gain better search engine placement.

SEO See *Search Engine Optimization*

Server A computer or operating system optimized to provide network services.

Shopping Cart An application that tracks items for purchase online.

SMTP *Simple Mail Transport Protocol* Protocol used in the delivery and receipt of email.

Spam Zombie A computer that has been compromised and sends unsolicited email.

SSL –Security Certificate necessary for ecommerce sites.

Static IP An IP address that does not change.

Static Website A brochure type website that contains content that rarely changes.

Style Sheet is an external list of CSS styles. See *Cascading Style Sheet*

Syntax The actual language and characters used in a programming language as opposed to programming logic.

Table A grid of rows and columns comprising cells

TCP/IP *Transmission Control Protocol/Internet Protocol* the underlying protocol of the Internet

Text Editor An application that can be used to manipulate simple text.

Top Level Domain Also known as a *TLD*. The main domain name extensions such as .com, .net, .org, etc...

UDP Also known as *User Datagram Protocol* a protocol that requires no confirmation of packet receipt. Commonly used with streaming media.

UNIX™ A computer operating system.

Visual Basic™ A programming language published by Microsoft®

VB™ See *Visual Basic*

VBScript™ A scripting language based on Visual Basic™

Viral Marketing A marketing campaign based on word of mouth. Typically involves a popular Internet phenomenon.

Virtual Shared Server Commonly used to run multiple websites independently on the same web server.

W3C See *World Wide Web Consortium.*

W3C Compliance Achieved with a website meets with the World Wide Web Consortium guidelines for website construction.

Web Application An application that is run on a web server

Web Form A form on a website that is typically used to gather information.

Web hosting server A server optimized to serve web sites.

Web host A web hosting services provider

Web space –This determines how much content you will be able to store on your site.

White Hats –Also known as White Hat Hackers. Hackers that are attempting to gain access to networks, websites, applications, etc... to expose security flaws, exploits or other legitimate issues.

White List A list of known legitimate mail servers that can bypass normal security kept by a mail server.

WYSIWYG Acronym for *what you see is what you get.* Typically associated with a application interface that allows the developer to see and/or manipulate the end result of an application in development.

NOTES...

www.ingramcontent.com/pod-product-compliance
Lightning Source LLC
Chambersburg PA
CBHW071549080326
40690CB00056B/1195